THE ULTIMATE

INSANELY

SUPER HOT
CHILI
PEPPER

COOKBOOK

THE ULTIMATE

INSANELY

SUPER HOT
CHILI
PEPPER
COOKBOOK

MICHAEL HARWOOD

FALL
RIVER
PRESS

Project Editor: Martha Burley
Editorial Assistants: Carly Beckerman, Tanya Laughton
Designers: Susi Martin, Chris Taylor
Art Director: Michael Charles
Managing Editor: Donna Gregory
Publisher: James Tavendale
QTT.MACH

Fall River Press
122 Fifth Avenue
New York, NY 10011

ISBN: 978-1-4351-1707-5

Printed and bound in China by 1010 Printing International Ltd.

10 9 8 7 6 5 4 3 2 1

CONTENTS

INTRODUCTION

by Michael Harwood

They say that some like it hot and when it comes to our taste in food it seems that most of us like it even hotter.

Chili peppers have been used to add heat and flavor to many of the world's cuisines for centuries but it was Christopher Columbus who was one of the first Europeans to encounter these spicy little fruits in the Caribbean back in the 1400s. He named them "peppers" because they reminded him of the much-coveted Old World black peppercorns (at least in flavor, if not in appearance).

Engraving (later coloration) showing Christopher Columbus at Hispaniola, 1886

Later, through trade with Spanish and Portuguese colonies, the popularity of chilies spread from their origins in Central and South America via the Philippines to India, Korea, China, Thailand, and Japan. At first it may seem strange that some of the world's hottest countries have embraced the fiery chili but actually it makes perfect sense. In the baking heat a plate of Duck vindaloo which contains large amounts of chili will actually open up the pores and trigger the body's highly effective self-cooling system. However, the appeal of chilies is not limited to these hot-climate countries—the Hungarians have embraced paprika so enthusiastically in the form of their national dish Paprikash that they now consume an estimated 11 pounds per head every year!

There are over 200 different species of chili but not all are used for their heat. The species *Capsicum annuum* (see page 16) includes the humble bell pepper as well as the equally mild paprika pepper.

By looking at the broadness of a chili you can see how hot it is going to be.

The heat of chili peppers is officially measured in Scoville Heat Units (SHU), named after Lincoln Scoville, the US chemist who, in 1912, developed a measure of the heat given off by the active ingredient capsaicin. The actual heat is concentrated along the top or "shoulders" of the pod and as a rule of thumb you can tell how hot a chili is going to be by looking at this. For example, the broad-shouldered bell pepper has no heat at all whereas the tiny Thai bird's eye chili is very narrow and packs a real punch. In many cases green chilies are also hotter than red but currently with so many hybrids being developed it is wise to take a very careful nibble of your chosen chili before adding it to your food in any quantity.

If you do find you have added a little too much heat to your food do not reach for the water. The water reacts with the heat-giving chemical in the chili and simply makes it worse. The best way to douse the flames is to drink milk as the dairy fat has a soothing effect on the capsaicin. This is why cultures that use a lot of chilies in their cuisine automatically serve a dairy side dish with it: yogurt with Indian meals or sour cream on top of spicy Mexican nachos.

Once the pepper has been cut open you can minimize the heat by removing the white flesh surrounding the seeds as this contains the highest concentration of capsaicin. Of course, if you are looking for maximum impact you can simply leave this step out.

At the furthest end of the heat scale is the *naga jolokia,* which *The Guinness Book of Records* lists as the hottest chili in the world and has an eye watering SHU of 1,000,000. Pure capsaicin has 16 times that amount and would, of course, be completely inedible. It is, however, manufactured in spray form as a very effective way of fighting off grizzly bears in the Rocky Mountains of North America.

There are as many uses for chilies in the kitchen as there are varieties and they come in all shapes and sizes, all with their own flavors, heats, and nuances. There are hot ones, mild ones, sweet ones, green ones, and red ones and you can read all about the different kinds in the *Chili species* chapter (see page 14).

About the pepper

The fiery, berrylike little pepper which Christopher Columbus introduced to Europe on his return from his voyage to the New World eventually came to thrive in the soil of southern Europe. Later, Portuguese and Spanish explorers spread an even wider variety of chilies and peppers they had encountered on their voyages. Peppers and chilies have been eaten in the New World for more than 7,000 years—native cuisines such as the Aztec, Inca, and Zapotec are strongly based on them, and the basis for their reputedly magical powers originates with the Chavin culture in the Peruvian

Andes, which erected a huge monolith as a paean to them. But the cuisines of the Far East, Australia, Africa, Europe, and the Mediterranean, which owe so much of their distinctive vigor and flavor to these vegetables, have only known the plant since 1493, a relatively short period of time. Soon Hungarian food was red with paprika (a hot form of ground chilies), Italian food was rich with peppers, Indian curries were scorched with chilies, and African food too was fired with hot peppers. The cuisines of the Old World were truly transformed, and have never looked back.

Chilies can add full flavor to a main dish such as a Thai green curry or create a subtle back note to some more unexpected dishes such as our Chili, avocado, and lemon muffins (page 178) or Sweet and spicy poached pears (page 184). The ancient Aztecs and Mayans realized many thousands of years ago that the combination of chili and chocolate is indeed heavenly—no doubt they would have approved of our Chili and chocolate chip cupcakes (page 181).

So, whether you are a seasoned pepper addict or a chili novice, here are recipes gathered from all four corners of the globe to tantalize your taste buds and help you turn up the heat.

CHOOSING, PREPARING & STORING

Choosing

Like all fresh fruit and vegetables, freshest is best. Look for peppers that are firm, shiny, and smooth, with a thick flesh and bright color. If wrinkled or flabby, avoid them as they will not be so fresh.

All peppers start out green, unripe, then ripen to yellow or red. A green pepper should not be too dark in color for its particular variety or it may indicate a slight immaturity without full-flavor benefits. Green peppers of all types should be picked when they reach their full size, but before they start to turn color.

All peppers, sweet or hot, regardless of their color, should be free of blemishes as darkened areas can be an indication of interior mold. Although available all year round, peppers are at their best when picked at the height of their season (summer and fall).

Safety first

Chilies need to be respected—they pack a real punch in cuisine but can cause serious amounts of pain if they are not handled carefully in the kitchen. The culprit is capsaicin, the oily substance which gives them their fiery flavor. Here are some tips for chili-loving success:

- Capsaicin does not dissolve in water, so it is important to soap your hand thoroughly after working with chilies.
- Wearing latex gloves is also a good option, but remember to wash knives, chopping boards, and other utensils thoroughly.
- If you do have a reaction on your skin, rubbing the stinging spot with a little shortening may help. Burning lips, tongue, or throat can be eased by a swallow of milk, sour cream, or yogurt.
- Avoid drinking water, which will make the problem worse.

All peppers, even fiery hot ones, are delicious eaten raw. Cut off the stems and remove the inside seeds and membranes. Some complain that raw peppers are difficult to digest; it is the skins that are hard to digest for most—peel the skin from the pepper and the problem is usually resolved.

Enjoy chopped, diced, or sliced raw peppers as a snack, as crudités, in salads or sandwiches. Raw chilies, sliced thin, are marvelous in salads (like the Saffron rice and almond salad, page 149), or chopped into salsas and other spicy dishes.

Preparing

Chopped or sliced chilies can be added to dishes immediately, but there are wonderful ways to prepare them to get the best flavors. Peeling the tough skins from peppers makes them easier to eat and it concentrates the flavor of the pepper, giving it a more mature taste. You could do this by heating peppers, then allowing them to steam slightly —this results in a different, juicy texture that works well if the peppers are to be marinated or pickled.

Roasting

Roasting peppers over an open flame gives the additional bonus of a smoky scent. Peppers can be roasted in a hot oven, under the broiler, on the barbecue, or on the stove.

1 Skewer them with a two-tine fork and hold them over a medium flame, turning them occasionally, until evenly charred.

Removing the seeds

If a recipe recommends seeding a chili, cut off the stem end, split the pod open, and scrape out the seeds and membrane with a teaspoon. Rinse and gently pat dry with paper towels.

2 Place each charred pepper in a plastic bag or wrap, a bowl, or a pan with a tight-fitting cover.

3 Seal or cover and allow to cool for at least 10 minutes, preferably longer. They will deflate and shrivel but their skin will easily lift off, revealing silky, supple flesh underneath.

Drying

Mature fresh chilies can be easily dried. They can be ground to make chili powder, or soaked and puréed.

1 Thread the chilies onto a large length of strong white string using a large needle. Ensure you pierce each chili just below the stem.

2 Hang the string of chilies in a hot, dry room or on the side of a building in the sun for about a week.

Preserving

You can make peppery salsas, sauces, jellies, spreads, and pickles. Pickling is one of the favorites—great for complementing curries or jazzing up milder dishes. See *Super-hot salsas, marinades & pastes* (page 56) for a whole host of delicious recipes.

1 Wash peppers well, leaving the stalks and seeds intact. Arrange them in sterilized jars. Fill the jars with water, then pour off the water into a pitcher.

2 Pour off half the water in the pitcher and replace with vinegar. Add 3 tablespoons of salt. If using small chilies do the same. Put the mixture of vinegar, water, and sugar into a nonreactive saucepan and bring to a boil.

3 Reduce the heat, let simmer for 10 minutes, then let cool slightly for 20–30 minutes or until the liquid is warm but not hot.

4 Pour the warm liquid into the jars of peppers, making sure that the peppers are completely covered, as they absorb liquid into the hollow middles. Add more vinegar if needed. Refrigerate. They should be ready to eat in two weeks.

Chilies preserved in oil.

Storing

Raw, unblanched peppers can be kept for about
6 months, without olive oil, between sheets of waxed
paper and plastic wrap, in the freezer.

Roasted, peeled chilies can be frozen and kept in
the freezer for up to 6 months. Their heat will fade.
This is useful for whole chilies, such as poblanos,
or Anaheims, that may be too hot to eat. Put them
in a bag and freeze for a few days to tame the fire.
Defrosted peppers which have lost their flavor, on the
other hand, can be boosted by sprinkling them with
cayenne pepper and allowing them to marinate for a
few hours.

Chilies drying outside a house in Mexico.
A whole dry chili can pack a punch in a casserole.

CHILI SPECIES

The following directory divides chili peppers into their main families, and discusses the differences of their major varieties in size, flavor, color, and heat. Use the key below to gauge heat levels for the perfect spice sensation.

🌶	A little heat
🌶🌶	Starting to sizzle
🌶🌶🌶	Too hot to handle
🌶🌶🌶🌶	Not for the fainthearted
🌶🌶🌶🌶🌶	Eye-wateringly hot
🌶🌶🌶🌶🌶	Danger—extreme heat

CAPSICUM ANNUUM

Capsicum annuum
"Anaheim"

Scoville rating:
1,000–10,000

The Anaheim, also called the California chili, is 5–7 inches long and 1 inch or so wide. It is one of the mildest members of the chili family, and a cousin of the New Mexico chili. Widely available fresh, probably second to the jalapeño, it is often canned and labeled simply "green chilies." It is also one of the most readily available dried chilies, when it turns deep burgundy in color. A mild California chili powder is made from the Anaheim, so when used in dishes like chili con carne, hotter chilies are usually added.

* Flavor: unique, crisp
* Heat: mild
* Plant height: 18–24 in. (45–60cm)
* Fruit color at maturity: red/green
* Fruit shape: elongated, pointed
* Fruit length: 5–7 in. (12.7–17.8cm)
* Fruit width: 1 in. (2.5cm)
* Fruit surface: smooth
* Alternatives: "New Mexico"

Capsicum annuum
"cayenne"

Scoville rating:
30,000–50,000

The cayenne is a bright red, thin, and pointed chili pepper, about 3–7 inches long. It is extremely hot, yet sweet, with a flavor that resembles that of Thai bird's eye chilies. It is a common ingredient in many Asian as well as Mexican dishes. It is most familiar dried and ground into cayenne pepper, sometimes called simply red pepper, which adds heat but not much flavor to any dish. These chilies are used for classic dried hanging decorations.

* Flavor: sweet
* Heat: hot
* Plant height: 24–29 in. (60–70cm)
* Fruit color at maturity: red
* Fruit shape: long, thin, sharply pointed
* Fruit length: 5–10 in. (12.7–25.5cm)
* Fruit width: / in. (1.3cm)
* Fruit surface: rough, uneven
* Alternatives: "habanero," "Thai," "serrano"

Capsicum annuum
"jalapeño"

Scoville rating:
2,000–5,000

This is the most widely available fresh chili in the U.S. Smooth, glossy, and usually 2–3 inches long, jalapeños are usually sold green, but turn red when ripe. Several raw and unseeded jalapeños added to a chili dish will turn up the heat considerably. Smoked jalapeños, or "chipotles," have a strong, smoky flavor, while pickled jalapeños, "jalapeños en escabeche," are usually used as a garnish. Dried jalapeños and jalapeño chili powder are both scarce.

* Flavor: rich, sweet
* Heat: moderate to hot
* Plant height: 24–48 in. (60–122cm)
* Fruit color at maturity: red/green
* Fruit shape: cylindrical, rounded tip
* Fruit length: 2–3 / in. (5–9cm)
* Fruit width: 1–1 / in. (2.5–3.8cm)
* Fruit surface: smooth, glossy
* Alternatives: "cuaresmeno," "serrano"

Green poblano chilies—although readily available dry, these sweet tasting fresh chilies are great additions to mild curries.

16

Originating from northern Latin America, *Capsicum annuum* is the most commonly cultivated chili pepper species, and comes in thousands of different varieties. These are believed to have been grown domestically in Mexico from as far back as 2500 BCE and the seeds taken back to Europe from the then-colonies of Spain and Portugal by Christopher Columbus.

Cayenne pepper plant at maturity.

Capsicum annuum
"pasilla"

Scoville rating:
1,000–1,500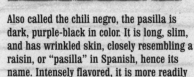

Also called the chili negro, the pasilla is dark, purple-black in color. It is long, slim, and has wrinkled skin, closely resembling a raisin, or "pasilla" in Spanish, hence its name. Intensely flavored, it is more readily available dried than fresh, and is often used in commercial chili powder blends.
The dried poblano is sometimes mislabeled as pasilla. Held up to the light, a dried poblano, or "ancho," is reddish, while the pasilla is brown-black, hotter, and not as sweet as the poblano.

* Flavor: intense, sweet, smoky
* Heat: mild to moderate
* Plant height: 22 in. (56cm)
* Fruit color at maturity: purple/black
* Fruit shape: thin, pointed
* Fruit length: 7 / in. (20cm)
* Fruit width 2 / in. (6cm)
* Fruit surface: wrinkled
* Alternatives: "mulato," "poblano"

Capsicum annuum
"poblano"

Scoville rating:
1,000–2,000

Green or red, this thick-fleshed chili is 4–5 inches long. A moderately spicy chili, the poblano has a complex, earthy flavor with hints of chocolate. Green chili stews are usually made with large quantities of poblanos, without making the stew too hot. In a hot chili, they are combined with hotter varieties of chilies. They are almost always peeled and roasted, and make delicious garnishes when roasted in strips called "rajas."

* Flavor: earthy, hints of chocolate
* Heat: mild to moderate
* Plant height: 24 in. (60cm)
* Fruit color at maturity: dark green/red/purple
* Fruit shape: heart
* Fruit length: 4–5 in. (10–12.5cm)
* Fruit width: 3 in. (7.6cm)
* Fruit surface: smooth
* Alternatives: "Anaheim," "bell pepper"

Capsicum annuum
"Thai/bird's eye"

Scoville rating:
100,000–175,000

This small but powerful chili seldom grows larger than 1–3 inches in length. It is a thin elongated green or red chili with a pointed end. Thin-fleshed with many seeds, it has a fierce heat. Grown in Thailand, Asia, and California, they are ideal for stir-fries and Asian dishes, when they are often mixed with the hot oil. These chilies are the subject of a Thai proverb pointing out the unexpected power of something so small.

* Flavor: potent, fiery
* Heat: very hot
* Plant height: 36 in. (90cm)
* Fruit color at maturity: red
* Fruit shape: curvy, pointed tip
* Fruit length: 1–3in. (2.5–7.6cm)
* Fruit width: / in. (1.3cm)
* Fruit surface: smooth
* Alternatives: "jalapeño"

CAPSICUM CHINENSE

Capsicum chinense
"ají dulce"

Scoville rating:
1–1,000

A good choice for those who like the flavor and aroma of Habanero peppers but find them too hot. Ají dulce has the same shape, size, color, and aroma as habanero, but is sweet, spicy, and delicious, with only a trace of heat. The fruits are highly aromatic and the flavor is unusual and complex, with overtones of black pepper and cilantro, and undertones of other spicy flavors. The pods themselves are approximately 1–2 inches long by 1–1 ¼ inches wide. The shape is tapering and the pods mature from pale green to orange and then red.

* Flavor: pungent, sweet
* Heat: very mild
* Plant height: 18–30 in. (45–75cm)
* Fruit color at maturity: red
* Fruit shape: tapered
* Fruit length: 1–2 in. (2.5–5cm)
* Fruit width: 1 in. (2.5cm)
* Fruit surface: shallow wrinkles
* Alternatives: "poblano"

Capsicum chinense
"Dorset naga"

Scoville rating:
850,000–1,000,000

This explosively hot specimen is the current record holder for the world's hottest chili. The Dorset variety was cultivated by a couple of horticultural enthusiasts in Dorset, England, from a Bangladeshi variety. They are green or red, slightly wrinkled and cone-shaped, about 1 inch wide at the stem end and up to 3½ inches long, tapering to a pointy tip. The flesh is very thin and despite their colossal heat, their flavor is also powerfully fruity.

* Flavor: aromatic, savory
* Heat: extremely hot
* Plant height: 18–47 in. (45–120cm)
* Fruit color at maturity: red
* Fruit shape: conical
* Fruit length: 2½–3½ in. (6–8.5cm)
* Fruit width: 1–1¼ in. (2.5–3cm)
* Fruit surface: rough, uneven
* Alternatives: "habanero"

Capsicum chinense
"jacquin" cv. datil

Scoville rating:
100,000–250,000

The datil was brought to the USA from the West Indies during the colonial period (1565–1821), though there is a myth that Minorcans fleeing Spain brought it with them. However, it was Minorcans who gave it its name—"datil," which means "date" in Catalan—after the date fruit which grows in Spain. The little, golden, wrinkled peppers look somewhat like fresh dates before the dates are harvested.

* Flavor: unique, aromatic
* Heat: very hot
* Plant height: 18–30 in. (45–75cm)
* Fruit color at maturity: green/golden-yellow
* Fruit shape: elongated, pointed
* Fruit length: ½–4 in. (1.5–10cm)
* Fruit width: 1 in. (2.5cm)
* Fruit surface: shallow wrinkles
* Alternatives: "habanero," "Scotch bonnet"

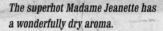

The superhot Madame Jeanette has a wonderfully dry aroma.

Capsicum chinense or "Chinese capsicum" is something of a misnomer since all capsica originate in the New World, not the Far East. Nikolaus Joseph von Jacquin, an Austrian botanist who saw the chilies in Central America, named the species erroneously in 1776, because he believed that they originated in China.

The fiery Dorset naga.

Capsicum chinense
"jacquin" cv. habanero

Scoville rating:
80,000–300,000

Habaneros used to hold the trophy for the world's hottest chili, though now the naga family reigns. The name means "from Havana," and they are especially widespread in the Yucatan peninsula of Mexico, just a short hop over the water from Cuba. Although near the top of the heat scale, they taste intensely fruity. Habaneros and Scotch bonnet chilies look and taste almost identical. Both are much loved all over Latin America, especially in the Caribbean.

* Flavor: intensely fruity
* Heat: very hot
* Plant height: 18–47 in. (45–120cm)
* Fruit color at maturity: green/orange/red
* Fruit shape: wavy lantern
* Fruit length: 2 / –3 / in. (6–8.5cm)
* Fruit width: 1 in. (2.5cm)
* Fruit surface: smooth
* Alternatives: "sweet datil"

Capsicum chinense
"habanero chocolate"

Scoville rating:
800,000–1,000,000

Black habanero is an alternative name often used to describe the dark brown variety of habanero chilies. Tiny slivers can have a dramatic effect. Gourmets delight in its fiery heat and unusual flavor. They take much longer to grow than other habanero chili varieties but are considered to be worth the wait. In a dried form they can be preserved for long periods of time and can be reconstituted in water.

* Flavor: exotic and sweet
* Heat: extremely hot
* Plant height: 18–47 in. (45–120cm)
* Fruit color at maturity: chocolate brown
* Fruit shape: shrunken lantern/heart-shaped
* Fruit length: 1 / –2 in. (4–5cm)
* Fruit width: 1 / in. (4cm)
* Fruit surface: wrinkled
* Alternatives: "habanero," "Scotch bonnet"

Capsicum chinense
"Madame Jeanette"

Scoville rating:
800,000–1,000,000

Also known as Surinam yellow, this is a real firecracker, a pure heat hit. Very hot, and with little accompanying flavor, the Madame Jeanette chili is closely related to the habanero chili and Scotch bonnet. A Madame Jeanette is just as hot as a habanero, but has a bit more of that typical dry aroma that gives Surinam dishes their characteristic and unique taste.

* Flavor: dry, savory
* Heat: extremely hot
* Plant height: 12–15 in. (30–45cm)
* Fruit color at maturity: yellow
* Fruit shape: collapsed oblong
* Fruit length: 3–4 in. (10–12cm)
* Fruit width: 1 / in. (4cm)
* Fruit surface: smooth
* Alternatives: "habanero," "Scotch bonnet"

CAPSICUM FRUTESCENS

Capsicum frutescens
"Tabasco"

Scoville rating:
50,000–100,000

Named after the Mexican state of Tabasco, this variety of chili pepper is grown in large quantities in Louisiana and Central and South America. The tabasco chili is about 1½ inches long, thin-fleshed with a strong, biting heat. Initially pale yellow-green, turning yellow and orange before ripening to bright red, it is used mainly for making the famous Tabasco sauce. This mixture of chili, salt, and vinegar remains the most successful chili sauce ever made. The tabasco plant is also very decorative, and it is easy to grow in warm climates.

* Flavor: salty, strong
* Heat: very hot
* Plant height: 40 in. (100cm)
* Fruit color at maturity: red
* Fruit shape: short cylinder, tapered
* Fruit length: 1½ in. (4cm)
* Fruit width: ½ in. (1.3cm)
* Fruit surface: smooth
* Alternatives: "malagueta"

Capsicum frutescens
"Japone"

Scoville rating:
20,000–25,000

The Japone chili is a small, pointed chili, about 2 inches long and ½ inch wide. The Japone is similar in appearance to the chili de arbol but has thicker walls. Dried, they are medium hot and commonly used in Japanese, Chinese, and Thai dishes, especially stir-fries. It is the principal chili pepper used in the famous Szechwan dishes, and is also a great addition to chili con carne or crushed into a red chili sauce.

* Flavor: distinctive, tangy
* Heat: mild to moderate
* Plant height: 36–50 in. (90–120cm)
* Fruit color: at maturity red
* Fruit shape: thin, pointed
* Fruit length: 2 in. (5cm)
* Fruit width: ½ in. (1.25cm)
* Fruit surface: smooth
* Alternatives: "de arbol"

Capsicum frutescens
"pequin/bird pepper"

Scoville rating:
50,000–100,000

The pequin (meaning little) chili or "bird pepper," is the smallest chili pepper but also one of the hottest. They grow in the highlands of Mexico and are commonly eaten by birds, hence their nickname. Oval shaped, averaging no more than ¼–½ inch long and ¼ inch wide, they have a complex and highly pungent taste, often described as nutty, smoky, even citrusy. They are most commonly used in salsas, sauces, and stews.

* Flavor: smoky, nutty, citrusy
* Heat: Hot
* Plant height: 36–48 in. (90–120cm)
* Fruit color at maturity: bright orange/red
* Fruit shape: oval, elongated, tapered
* Fruit length: ½–¾ in. (1.5–2cm)
* Fruit width: ¼ in. (0.5cm)
* Fruit surface: smooth
* Alternatives: "tepin," "cayenne," "cascabel"

Decorative Tabasco peppers maturing on the plant.

The chilies from this sub-species *frutescens*, meaning shrubby or bushy, grow on plants between one and four feet high depending on climatic conditions. The *frutescens* chili species is quite hot, measuring between 20,000 and 100,000 Scoville Heat Units and the pods are most commonly used to make hot sauces, or dried for adding to stir-fried dishes.

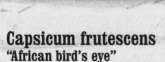

Malagueta chilies are native to Brazil.

Capsicum frutescens
"African bird's eye"

Scoville rating:
50,000–175,000

Small and extremely spicy, this chili is also known as the "African devil" or "African red devil," and is the North African equivalent of the cayenne pepper. Tapered to a blunt point, it is usually around 1 inch long and green, ripening to a bright red-purple. It is often referred to as "piri piri" and used in the making of sauces and marinades, especially in Portuguese cuisine. Fresh red pods are 2–3 times hotter than the green fruit and, when dried, are 10 times hotter again!

* Flavor: pungent, sweet
* Heat: very hot
* Plant height 42 in. (106cm)
* Fruit color: bright red/purple
* Fruit shape: tapered, pointed tip
* Fruit length: 1 in. (2.5cm)
* Fruit width: ¼ in. (6mm)
* Fruit surface: smooth, dented
* Alternatives: "cayenne"

Capsicum frutescens
"malagueta"

Scoville rating:
60,000–100,000

Grown semi-wild in the Amazon basin in Brazil, this potent chili is most commonly used to season regional dishes in Brazil and Mozambique, and in Portugal where it is most often used to season poultry dishes. Extremely potent in flavor and heat, this chili is believed to have got its name from the unrelated melegueta pepper from West Africa. It is about 2 inches long and bright red when mature.

* Flavor: pungent, sweet
* Heat: very hot
* Plant height: 42 in. (106cm)
* Fruit color at maturity: bright red/purple
* Fruit shape: tapered, pointed tip
* Fruit length: 2 in. (5cm)
* Fruit width: ¼ in. (6mm)
* Fruit surface: smooth, dented
* Alternatives: "cayenne"

Capsicum frutescens
"naga jolokia"

Scoville rating:
855,000–1,000,000

Also known as the bhut jolokia, ghost chili, and naga morich, this chili grows predominanly in India, Bangladesh, and Sri Lanka. It has competed with the "red savina" chili as the hottest chili in the world, reaching a reported scorching 855,000 units on the Scoville scale in 2000. In 2007, the Guiness World Records certified it as the hottest chili pepper on Earth. It measures around 2½ inches and 1¼ inches wide, and is orange/red when ripe.

* Flavor: strong, salty
* Heat: dangerously hot
* Plant height: 18–47 in. (45–120cm)
* Fruit color at maturity: orange/red
* Fruit shape: wavy lantern, pointed tip
* Fruit length: 2½ in. (6.4cm)
* Fruit width: 1¼ in. (3.2cm)
* Fruit surface: rough, dented
* Alternative: "red savina"

CAPSICUM PUBESCENS

Capsicum pubescens
"rocoto"

Scoville rating:
40,000–100,000

The rocoto has been cultivated in Peru and Bolivia for thousands of years. It has thick walls like the bell pepper, is on average about 2 / inches long, and is the only pepper to have black seeds. Rocoto is one of the oldest domesticated peppers and comes in two varieties, one turning from green to red, and the other more flavorful variety common in the Caribbean and Mexico, turning from green to orange. In Peru, rocotos are the most common hot peppers and are used to spice up most of their dishes. This chili is never used in its dry form.

* Flavor: unique, apple-like taste
* Heat: moderate to quite hot
* Plant height: 12–72 in. (30–180cm)
* Fruit color at maturity: red/orange
* Fruit shape: wavy lantern
* Fruit length: 2 / in. (6.4cm)
* Fruit width: 1 in. (2.5cm)
* Fruit surface: smooth
* Alternatives: "manzano"

Capsicum pubescens
"manzano"

Scoville rating:
50,000–250,000

Originally from South America, the manzano chili is named after its resemblence to a "manzano," meaning apple in Spanish. It is more resistant to lower temperatures and is therefore, grown in cooler climates. Turning to a yellowy-orange color when ripe, this relation of the South American rocoto pepper has the same thick, black pods, which are difficult to dry. The manzano is therefore, most often used fresh in hot salsas.

* Flavor: pungent
* Heat: hot to very hot
* Plant height: 12–72 in. (30–180cm)
* Fruit color at maturity yellow/orange
* Fruit shape spherical
* Fruit length 2 in. (5cm)
* Fruit width 2 in. (5cm)
* Fruit surface smooth
* Alternatives: "rocoto"

Capsicum pubescens
"perón rojo"

Scoville rating:
100,000–350,000

Named "perón rojo" in Spanish after its pear-like shape, this chili pepper is native to the Michoacan region of Mexico and the Central American rainforest. Unlike other, more fragile peppers, the perón rojo survives harsh winters with little sun. It only requires shelter from the wind, and grows into a large, ornate plant with purple flowers. Delicious shaved finely into fresh salads, this hot pepper is also used as a tequila shot glass.

* Flavor: sweet
* Heat: extremely hot
* Plant height: 24–36 in. (60–90cm)
* Fruit color at maturity: red
* Fruit shape: bell
* Fruit length: 2 in. (5cm)
* Fruit width: 1 / in. (3.25cm)
* Fruit surface: smooth, glossy
* Alternatives: "habanero"

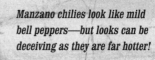

Manzano chilies look like mild bell peppers—but looks can be deceiving as they are far hotter!

Capsicum pubescens, or "hairy peppers," are often grown at high altitudes in tropical countries due to the fine layer of hair that covers its plant. The chilies have unique black seeds and cannot be cross-pollinated with other species, resulting in a lack of pod diversity. Possibly due to its very early domestication, there are no wild forms left and it is thought to be one of the oldest domesticated plants in the Americas.

Under-ripe rocoto chilies.

Capsicum pubescens
"Cuzco"

Scoville rating:
40,000–100,000

An ancient chili pepper growing in Peru for almost 8,000 years, the Cuzco pepper is named for Peru's oldest city, the capital of the Incan empire. Native to the Andes, this pepper is rarely grown anywhere else. It cannot be cross-bred with any other species, and the fruit does not separate easily from the main plant, preventing it from spreading. Cuzco pepper is hot and sweet, perfect for salsas, and goes well with fish.

* Flavor: sweet with hot seeds
* Heat: moderate to quite hot
* Plant height: 12–72 in. (30–180cm)
* Fruit color at maturity: red/orange
* Fruit shape: wavy lantern
* Fruit length: 2½ in. (6.4cm)
* Fruit width: 1 in. (2.5cm)
* Fruit surface: smooth
* Alternatives: "manzano"

Capsicum pubescens
"canario"

Scoville rating:
40,000–50,000

Named for its yellow color, the canario chili pepper is a Peruvian variety known for its very hot flavor. Like its cousin, the rocoto, this pepper has black seeds and an apple-like shape. This is the hottest chili still large enough to stuff, and is often filled with a savory pork mixture including eggs and garlic. It is normally consumed in a fresh form (not dried) because the pods are too thick to dry properly.

* Flavor: sweet and crisp
* Heat: moderate to hot
* Plant height: 12–72 in. (30–180cm)
* Fruit color at maturity: yellow
* Fruit shape: spherical
* Fruit length: 2 in. (5cm)
* Fruit width: 2 in. (5cm)
* Fruit surface: smooth
* Alternatives: "manzano"

Capsicum pubescens
"ají mongol"

Scoville rating:
1,500–2,000

A small plant that bears drooping apple-shaped red fruit, the ají mongol is an unusual shape for pubescens. It is also very rare, and often mistaken for a separate variety because the seeds are dark brown instead of black. Originating from Venezuela, this chili has a much milder flavor than its Mexican and Peruvian counterparts. A very good pepper for stuffing, the ají mongol variety is a favorite for salads and mild salsas.

* Flavor: sweet and tangy
* Heat: mild
* Plant height: 18 in. (45cm)
* Fruit color at maturity: red
* Fruit shape: spherical
* Fruit length: 2½ in. (6.4cm)
* Fruit width: 2½ in. (6.4cm)
* Fruit surface: smooth
* Alternatives: "perón rojo"

CAPSICUM BACCATUM

Capsicum baccatum
"ají amarillo"

Scoville rating:
40,000–50,000

Literally meaning "yellow chili" in Spanish, these chilies actually turn an orange color when fully ripe. Grown in South America, predominantly Peru, they are fairly hot with a slightly fruity, citrus flavor and are best used in salsa, ceviche, sauces, or pickles. They are often ground into a powder or made into a chili paste, and then added to a variety of dishes. These attractive chilies were apparently described by the famous Peruvian chef Gastón Acurio as the most important ingredient in Peruvian cooking.

* Flavor: fruity, citrusy
* Heat: moderate to hot
* Plant height: 36 in. (90cm)
* Fruit color at maturity: orange
* Fruit shape: extended wavy cone
* Fruit length: 4–6 in. (10–15.25cm)
* Fruit width: / –1 in. (2–3cm)
* Fruit surface: smooth, wavy
* Alternatives: "habanero," "serrano"

Capsicum baccatum
"ají cereza"

Scoville rating:
30,000–40,000

Meaning "cherry chili" in Spanish, these small, round chilies closely resemble cherries, and grow upright on their tall, sprawling chili plants. Native to the Peruvian jungle, this tiny chili has a strong, pungent flavor and turns from green to a rich red color when fully ripened. There are no domestic growers, so this chili is rare outside of Peru, though seeds, dried, or powdered cereza are readily available online.

* Flavor: pungent, rich
* Heat: mild to moderate
* Plant height: 24–36 in. (60–90cm)
* Fruit color at maturity: deep red
* Fruit shape: small sphere
* Fruit length: 1 in. (2.5cm)
* Fruit width: 1 in. (2.5cm)
* Fruit surface: smooth
* Alternatives: "ají orchid"

Capsicum baccatum
"ají limon"

Scoville rating:
30,000–50,000

Legend has it the "ají limon" was named after the Peruvian city of Lima. This bright yellow chili is now appropriately named "lemon pepper," and is one of the most flavorful of the Andean peppers. They have a distinctive floral, citrusy flavor, and an intense heat. The chili's complex flavors really stand out when used in salsas in particular, and its lemony overtones also make it very suitable for fish, seafood, and poultry dishes.

* Flavor: floral, citrusy
* Heat: moderate to hot
* Plant height: 36 in. (90cm)
* Fruit color at maturity: ivory/yellow
* Fruit shape: elongated, flattened, tapered
* Fruit length: 1 / –2 / in. (4–7cm)
* Fruit width: / in. (2cm)
* Fruit surface: smooth, wavy
* Alternatives: "ají amarillo"

A dry ají pepper—popular in Italian cooking.

Throughout their native lands—Peru, Brazil, Colombia, Ecuador, Bolivia, and Argentina—the *Capsicum baccatum* chili varieties are commonly referred to as "ají," and used fresh in dishes for their fruity, and often citrusy flavor. With their name "baccatum" meaning berrylike, these chilies vary in size and shape but are usually yellow and orange.

The Christmas bell is one of the most flavorful chilies.

Capsicum baccatum
"criolla sella"

Scoville rating:
100,000–150,000

Originating from Bolivia, this chili is very hot and is great for adding to salsas and salads. These chilies reach up to 3 inches in length and taper to a point. The thin flesh also makes it ideal for drying. Growing up to 2 feet high and blooming with white and yellow flowers, this *Capsicum baccatum* also makes a decorative ornate plant for your home. In warm conditions, the criolla sella will bloom and fruit well.

* Flavor: fruity, citrusy
* Heat: very hot
* Plant height: 60 in. (152cm)
* Fruit color at maturity: yellow-orange
* Fruit shape: cylindrical, tapered
* Fruit length: 2–3 in. (5–7.6cm)
* Fruit width: ½ in. (1.3cm)
* Fruit surface: smooth
* Alternatives: "bubba"

Capsicum baccatum
"Christmas bell"

Scoville rating:
100–500

Shaped similar to a bell-like Christmas decoration, this unusual chili comes from the Netherlands. It turns from green to a bright red when fully ripe. The Christmas bell is also known as "joker's hat" and "balloon," and grows up to 2¼ inches long on a very tall plant. Often pickled and popular in Italian cooking, the Christmas bell has a spicy, fruity flavor that goes well with fish, light sauces, or served as antipasti.

* Flavor: sweet, fruity, juicy
* Heat: very mild
* Plant height: 60 in. (152cm)
* Fruit color at maturity: bright red
* Fruit shape: bell
* Fruit length: 2 in. (2.5cm)
* Fruit width: 2½ in. (6.34cm)
* Fruit surface: smooth, glossy
* Alternatives: "sweet datil"

Capsicum baccatum
"Brazilian starfish"

Scoville rating:
40,000–50,000

This uniquely-shaped chili pepper is a variety in high demand. The star-like fruit turns from green/orange to bright red when mature, and it has a very pungent aroma. Native to Brazil, these chilies are sometimes called "sand dollars," and are perfect stuffed with cream cheese or used in salsas. The Brazilian starfish plant is very decorative, but will only flourish in warm, slightly humid climates or greenhouses.

* Flavor: savory, tangy
* Heat: moderate to hot
* Plant height: 36 in. (90cm)
* Fruit color at maturity: bright red
* Fruit shape: star
* Fruit length: 2 in. (5cm)
* Fruit width: 2 in. (5cm)
* Fruit surface: smooth, ribbed
* Alternatives: "bi-bell"

GROWING YOUR OWN CHILIES

Growing chilies is fun, for their sheer variety. Each time you see an unusual chili species, pick one up, dry the seeds, and when the time comes, sow them. It's a treat to see the range of colors, textures, heat, and flavors you will find blooming in your garden.

Chili plants start producing flowers when they are 5–6 inches (12–15cm) tall. If growing them indoors, help them to pollinate either by giving the plants a gentle shake every so often or by using a cotton swab or light brush. If you are trying to keep the varieties pure to save seeds, don't use the same brush or cotton swab on different plants.

The peppers' fire and pungency depend on the weather and sun: the hotter and brighter the sun, the spicier the pepper. A little stress on the plant, such as letting it dry out just a little too far once or twice, can also increase its heat.

During the season, which will depend on the region where you live, you can pick your peppers and chilies as you like, before they grow too large, and eat them fresh. When the first frosts strike, pick the peppers that remain on the plants and dry them out for use through the winter.

APPETIZERS & SOUPS

MEDIUM
SPICE

COCONUT SOUP
INFUSED WITH LEMONGRASS

The heat from the chilies gives this soup extra warmth. This soup will keep in the refrigerator for up to two days or in the freezer for up to a month.

INGREDIENTS

- 2 pints chicken stock
- 4 chicken breasts, boneless, skinless
- 3 stalks lemongrass, sliced thinly (use the hearts only)
- 4 oz galangal, sliced thinly
- 4 oz enoki mushrooms
- 2 shallots, sliced thinly
- 3 kaffir lime leaves, torn
- large bunch cilantro, chopped coarsely
- 1 tbsp bird's eye chilies, chopped
- 4 tbsp fish sauce
- 3 tbsp lime juice
- 1 tsp sugar
- 4 tbsp coconut milk

1. In a pan, bring the stock to a boil. Add chicken breasts and poach for 3–5 minutes. Remove the chicken breasts from the stock, cut into cubes and set aside.

2. Put all the remaining ingredients into the stock and boil for about 10 minutes.

3. Add the chicken to the stock and turn the heat low, simmering for about 3 minutes. Remove the kaffir lime leaves and galangal pieces before serving.

SERVES 4

32 Manchego cheese with chili

PREP TIME
5 mins
COOKING TIME
2 hours

MILD SPICE

MANCHEGO CHEESE WITH CHILI

This dish, also known as *Quejo Manchego con Salsa Picante*, is great as a spicy alternative snack to the traditional cheese on cocktail sticks at parties.

INGREDIENTS

- 6 poblano chilies, deseeded and chopped
- 8 fl. oz olive oil
- salt and freshly ground pepper
- 9 oz Manchego cheese
- lime wedges, to serve

1. Blend the chilies with the olive oil, adding a good pinch each of salt and pepper.
2. Cut the cheese into small cubes. Pour the oil over the cheese and marinate for at least 2 hours.
3. Serve with lime wedges.

SERVES 4

PREP TIME
10 mins

COOKING TIME
20 mins

MILD
SPICE

FIERY PUMPKIN DIP

This glorious orange dip offers a rich combination of sweet, spicy, fiery, and sour flavors. But be warned—once you start dipping, it's hard to stop. You could try omitting the chili and adding 1 teaspoon harissa paste (page 58) and 1 teaspoon ground cumin.

INGREDIENTS

- 1 lb 5 oz butternut squash or pumpkin, deseeded, peeled, and cut into chunks
- 2 tbsp olive oil
- salt and ground pepper
- 1 garlic clove, peeled and minced
- 1 tsp grated fresh gingerroot
- 1 pasilla chili, seeded and finely chopped
- juice of ½ lime

1. Preheat the oven to 400°F (200°C). Put the squash or pumpkin in a baking dish, drizzle with 1 tablespoon of the oil, and season with salt and pepper. Roast for about 20 minutes, tossing once or twice during cooking, until tender.

2. Transfer the squash or pumpkin to a food processor and add the garlic, ginger, chili, and remaining oil. Process until smooth, then briefly pulse with the lime juice and check the seasoning.

3. Scrape the dip into a bowl and serve hot, warm, or cold. (It will thicken on cooling, so give it a good stir before serving.)

SERVES 4

MEDIUM SPICE

CRAB CORN CHILIES RELLENOS

These chilies are stuffed with a rich combination of crab, corn, sour cream, and Monterey Jack cheese. They are dipped in an egg-white mixture, then fried until golden brown. Mild Anaheims and the moderately hot poblanos are best, but milder cubanelle could also be substituted.

INGREDIENTS

- 8 whole Anaheim or poblano chilies
- 6 oz crabmeat, picked over for bits of shell
- 3 oz chopped onion
- 5 oz corn kernels
- 4 fl. oz sour cream
- 2 tbsp chopped fresh cilantro
- ¼ tsp ground red pepper
- 1 tsp salt
- 8 oz Monterey Jack cheese, grated
- about 3 oz cornmeal for dredging
- 4 eggs, separated
- 2 tbsp flour
- ¼ tsp salt
- oil for frying
- salsa, to serve

1. Char the skins of the chilies under the broiler, turning until they are mostly black. As each chili is done, remove it from the heat and place it in a bag. When all the chilies are done, let them steam in the bag for 10 minutes. It will make them easier to peel.

2. Carefully peel off the blackened skin. Cut a slit down the length of each chili and remove the stem, seeds, and ribs. Set the chilies aside.

3. In a bowl, mix the crabmeat, onion, corn, sour cream, cilantro, ground red pepper, and salt. Put 3 tablespoons of grated cheese in each chili, then lightly stuff it with the crab mixture. The egg coating will help hold it together when it is fried. Dredge each chili in the cornmeal and shake off any excess.

4. In a medium bowl, beat the egg whites until soft peaks form.
In a second bowl, lightly beat the egg yolks with the flour and salt.
Fold the yolks into the whites.

5. Pour oil to a depth of ½ inch into a large skillet and heat. While the oil is heating, dip 2 or 3 chilies into the egg mixture, using a spatula to cover any bare spots. Carefully place each chili into the hot oil, adding only 2 or 3 at a time. Cook, turning once, until golden on all sides, for about 2 minutes. While the chilies are cooking, dip the next batch into the egg mixture.

6. Chilies rellenos can be kept in a warm oven until all are fried. Serve with salsa on the side.

SERVES 8

MILD SPICE

COLD AVOCADO SOUP

This cold soup is creamy and smooth, and although laced with chili, the inclusion of cream and milk will make your tolerance that little bit stronger.

~ INGREDIENTS ~

- 1–2 Anaheim chilies
- 1 tbsp olive oil
- 3 large ripe avocados
- 8 fl. oz chicken or vegetable stock
- 8 fl. oz light cream
- 8 fl. oz milk
- 1–2 tbsp lime juice
- salt and white pepper
- mint leaves, to garnish

1. Preheat the broiler to high. Cut each chili in half and discard the seeds. Place under the broiler, skin-side up, and drizzle with the oil. Broil for 5 minutes, or until the skin has blistered. Remove from the heat and let cool.

2. Discard the skin and membrane from the chili and roughly chop. Put into a food processor. Peel and pit the avocados, then roughly chop and put into the food processor with the stock. Blend to form a smooth purée.

3. With the machine still running at a slow speed, add the cream, then the milk.

4. Stir in the lime juice and seasoning to taste. Pour into a soup tureen and chill for at least 1 hour. Serve garnished with mint leaves.

SERVES 4

40 Tofu tossed with chili, chopped chives & peanuts

VERY HOT

TOFU
TOSSED WITH CHILI, CHOPPED CHIVES & PEANUTS

This makes for an extremely satisfying appetizer on its own or served as an accompaniment with another dish. Adjust the chilies to suit your taste.

⌇INGREDIENTS⌇

- 2 tbsp oyster sauce
- 2 tsp soy sauce
- 2 tbsp vegetable or sunflower oil
- 2 cloves garlic, peeled and minced
- 1-inch piece gingerroot, peeled and shredded
- 2 small bird's eye chilies, deseeded and finely sliced
- 1 small red bell pepper, julienned
- 1 bunch choy sum, cut into 2-inch lengths
- 8 long beans, cut into 2-inch lengths
- 6 oz fried tofu (bean curd), halved diagonally
- 1 tsp chopped chives, to serve
- 1 tsp peanuts, to serve

1. Combine the oyster sauce and soy sauce with 1 tablespoon of water and set aside.

2. Heat the oil in a wok or skillet, add the garlic, gingerroot, and chilies and fry for 1–2 minutes.

3. Add the bell pepper, choy sum, and beans. Stir-fry until the choy sum has slightly wilted and the beans and pepper are slightly soft, for about 2 minutes.

4. Add the tofu (bean curd) and oyster sauce mixture, toss for 3–4 minutes.

5. Remove from the heat, sprinkle with chopped chives and peanuts, and serve.

SERVES 4

CHILI CHEESE BREAD

MILD SPICE

Chilies and Cheddar cheese flavor this hearty yeast bread, which goes well with soup and salad. You can use canned chilies as a shortcut to roasting your own, but the flavor will not be as good.

~INGREDIENTS~

- 3 Anaheim, New Mexico green, or poblano chilies
- 4 fl. oz milk
- 2 tbsp butter
- ½ tsp salt
- 1 package active dry yeast (¼ oz)
- 2 fl. oz warm water
- 1 tsp sugar
- 10 oz all-purpose flour
- 1 egg, lightly beaten
- 4 oz grated Cheddar cheese

MAKES ONE LOAF

1. Preheat the broiler. Cut the chilies in half lengthwise, remove stems and seeds. Place under broiler, skin side up, and cook until skin blisters and turns mostly dark brown or black. Remove from broiler and place hot chilies in a bag or fold a pouch of aluminum foil around them to seal in the steam. Let them steam for 10 minutes, then peel off their skins and dice the chilies. This may be done up to a day in advance of making the bread.

2. Scald the milk. Add the butter and salt to the milk and let the mixture cool. It's fine if the butter does not melt completely.

3. Dissolve the yeast in the warm water and add the sugar. Let the yeast sit until it develops a foamy head, for about 10 minutes. When the milk mixture has cooled, combine it with the yeast mixture and pour the mixture into a

large bowl. Stir in 4 ounces of flour. Stir in egg, cheese, and chilies. Knead in a another 4 ounces of flour. Add the rest of the flour, knead lightly, then dump the mixture on to a floured surface. The dough does not need to be well blended when you dump it out. Continue kneading, adding a little flour if necessary, until the dough has been kneaded for a total of 10 minutes.

4. Place the dough in a greased bowl, then turn so all surfaces are lightly oiled. Cover the bowl and put it in a warm place. When the dough has doubled in volume, in about 1 hour, punch it down and knead lightly.

5. Let the dough rest while you lightly butter a 9-inch loaf pan. Shape the dough into a loaf and put it in the pan. Cover the pan and let it sit in a warm place until the dough doubles in volume again. About 20 minutes before the dough has fully risen, preheat the oven to 375°F (190°C). Bake the bread until the top is golden and sounds hollow when you tap it. This will take about 30 minutes.

SPICY CRAB SALAD

MEDIUM SPICE

In the Yucatan, where temperatures soar to almost unbearable heights, you will find salady dishes called *fiambre*—cool mixtures of hot, spicy ingredients. Often these are rolled up in fresh tortillas to make hot-weather tacos.

INGREDIENTS

- 3 shallots or ¼ red onion, finely chopped
- 1 fresh chili, such as jalapeño or serrano, chopped
- juice of ½ lime
- 1 tbsp white wine or fruit vinegar
- 1 tsp chopped fresh marjoram or ½ tsp chopped fresh oregano
- 1 tsp chopped fresh cilantro
- 1 tbsp olive oil
- 8–12 oz cooked crab meat
- fresh tortillas (optional)
- 1 avocado, peeled and sliced, to serve

1. Combine the shallots or onion with the chili, lime juice, vinegar, marjoram or oregano, cilantro, and olive oil.

2. Mix lightly with the crab.

3. Use to stuff fresh tortillas, if wished. Serve garnished with avocado.

SERVES 4

SPICY SAUSAGE AND BEAN SOUP

MEDIUM SPICE

This soup makes a hearty treat and is particularly good after a cold winter walk. It can be made ahead and reheated before serving. You could try adding 3 sliced bottled roast bell peppers with the whole borlotti beans.

❧INGREDIENTS❧

- 2 tbsp olive oil
- 5 good-quality pork sausages
- 1 onion, chopped
- 2 garlic cloves, finely chopped
- 1½ Cuzco or manzano chilies, deseeded and chopped
- 14-oz can chopped tomatoes
- 1½ pints beef or chicken stock
- 2 x 14-oz cans cranberry beans or cannellini beans, drained and rinsed
- salt and ground pepper
- 2 tbsp chopped fresh parsley

1. Heat the oil in a large saucepan. Add the sausages, brown them all over, and then remove. Add the onion, garlic, and chilies to the pan, and fry gently for 3 minutes.

2. Cut the sausages into thick slices and return them to the pan, adding the tomatoes and stock. Bring to a boil, then reduce the heat, cover, and simmer gently for 20 minutes.

3. Put half the beans in a food processor or blender and add a couple of ladlefuls of the soup stock. Process until smooth, then stir the purée into the soup with the remaining beans, and simmer for a further 10 minutes. Add salt and pepper to taste, and stir in the parsley before serving the soup.

SERVES 4

48 Red-hot spicy chickpea & pasta soup

PREP TIME
10 mins
COOKING TIME
30 mins

RED-HOT SPICY
CHICKPEA &
PASTA SOUP

VERY HOT

This chunky, wholesome soup has a real bite—making it perfect for serving on a cold day when you really need to warm yourself up. Why not try green chilies in place of the red, for an even spicier flavor.

INGREDIENTS

- 2 tbsp olive oil
- 3 red chilies like ají dulce or habanero, deseeded and chopped
- 3 garlic cloves, peeled and minced
- 6 ripe tomatoes, peeled and chopped
- 2 pints vegetable or chicken stock
- 14-oz can chickpeas, drained and rinsed
- 4 oz small pasta shapes
- bunch of scallions, sliced
- 1 tbsp chopped fresh mint, plus extra to garnish
- salt
- Parmesan cheese shavings, to garnish

1. Heat the oil in a large saucepan. Add the chilies and garlic, and cook gently for 2 minutes. Stir in the tomatoes, stock, and chickpeas, and bring to a boil. Reduce the heat, cover, and simmer for about 20 minutes.

2. Add the pasta to the soup and simmer for another 5 minutes, until tender. Stir in the scallions, mint, and salt to taste. Ladle the soup into bowls and serve immediately, sprinkled with the remaining mint and the Parmesan shavings.

SERVES 6

MEDIUM
SPICE

SOFT BEEF
TACOS WITH SALSA

Tacos have gone so mainstream that many families have a regular "taco night." Fresh, homemade tortillas make all the difference, as do fresh fillings and accompaniments. These soft beef tacos make a great snack at parties.

⌐INGREDIENTS⌐

- 1 lb ground beef
- 1 cup chopped onion
- 2 cloves garlic, minced
- 2 tbsp taco seasoning
- 1 cup bottled chipotle mojo marinade made from jalapeños
- 14-oz can red kidney beans
- soft corn tortillas
- salsa cruda or salsa (page 65)
- chopped fresh cilantro, to garnish

1. In a skillet over medium-high heat, brown the ground beef, onion, and garlic together.

2. Add the taco seasoning and chipotle mojo marinade. Add the kidney beans. Let simmer for 5 minutes.

3. To serve, place a spoonful of taco meat in the center of each tortilla. Top with salsa and the chopped cilantro.

SERVES 10 AS SNACK

VERY HOT

SPICY DIP WITH MACKEREL

Mackerel has a strong, smoky flavor which is complemented beautifully by a spark of fresh chilies. Perfect for dipping with carrot sticks or chips, this is party food that won't go unnoticed!

⌇INGREDIENTS⌇

- 3 x 4 oz baby mackerel, cleaned and gutted
- 1½ tsp salt
- ½ tbsp shrimp paste
- 2 tbsp dried shrimp, pounded fine
- 1 tbsp sliced garlic
- 2 small eggplants, peeled
- 15 fresh small whole pequin or habañero chilies
- 6 pea-sized eggplants or 2 oz fresh green peas
- 2 tbsp lemon juice
- 1 tbsp fish sauce
- 4 fl. oz peanut or corn oil
- 1 large fresh chili, sliced into rounds

1. Rub the mackerel inside and out with the salt and leave in a cool place for 1 hour.

2. Wrap the shrimp paste in foil and heat in a pan over high heat for 5 minutes (or roast in a 350°F/175°C oven for 8 minutes), then remove and unwrap.

3. Pound the shrimp paste, dried shrimp, garlic, and eggplant together with a mortar and pestle or in a blender. Add the small chilies, pound lightly, then mix in the remaining eggplants or peas, lemon juice, and fish sauce.

4. Heat the oil in a skillet over a medium heat and fry the fish for 6–8 minutes on each side —the flesh should be tender but firm and white in the center. Serve the fish with the dip, garnished with sliced chili.

BEYA KYAW
SPLIT PEA FRITTERS

A popular way to start a Burmese meal is to offer a selection of small dishes, known locally as *tolee molee* or "bits and pieces." Beya kyaw is one of these small dishes. Try adding 2 tablespoons of fresh cilantro to the fritter mixture.

PREP TIME
12 hours
COOKING TIME
10 mins

INGREDIENTS

- 8 oz yellow split peas
- 1 tbsp besan (chickpea flour) or all-purpose whole-wheat flour
- 1 small onion, peeled and very finely chopped
- ½ tsp turmeric
- 1 garlic clove, peeled and minced
- ½ tsp chili powder
- 1 tsp baking powder
- salt and pepper
- oil, for deep-frying

1. Place the split peas in a bowl, cover with cold water, and soak for 12 hours or overnight. Drain.

2. In a food processor, grind the split peas to a fine meal. Transfer to a bowl and stir in the flour, onion, turmeric, garlic, chili, baking powder, and seasoning. Beat until the mixture is light and fluffy.

3. Heat the oil in a wok or large pan to 375°F (190°C). Roll the mixture into walnut-sized balls and fry in two or three batches until golden brown.

4. Drain on paper towels and serve warm with sesame dipping sauce (see page 81).

HOT CHILI SQUID SOUP

Chilies, tomatoes, and squid seem to be a combination made in heaven, and they are divine in this light tomato broth. If you like garlic, try replacing the shallots with 3 garlic cloves.

⸙ INGREDIENTS ⸙

- 6 squid, cleaned
- juice of 1 lemon
- 3 tbsp olive oil
- 3 shallots, finely chopped
- 2 bird's eye chilies, deseeded and chopped
- 1 lb ripe tomatoes, peeled, deseeded, and chopped
- 3 pints fish or vegetable stock
- 1 tbsp tomato paste
- ½ tsp ground cinnamon
- pinch of light brown sugar
- salt and ground pepper
- 1 tbsp chopped fresh mint

1. Separate the tentacles from the squid in one piece. Discard the head. Slice the bodies into rings and put in a bowl with the tentacles and lemon juice. Cover and chill for 30 minutes.

2. Heat 2 tablespoons of the oil in a large saucepan. Add the shallots and chilies, and cook gently for 2 minutes. Add the tomatoes, stock, tomato paste, and cinnamon. Bring to a boil, reduce heat, cover, and simmer for 10 minutes. Process the soup in a blender until smooth, then return it to the pan. Add sugar and salt and pepper to taste. Keep warm.

3. Drain the squid, pat dry on paper towels, then season with salt and pepper. Heat the remaining oil in a nonstick skillet. Fry the squid for 1 minute, until just cooked. Ladle the soup into bowls, spoon the squid on top, sprinkle with fresh mint, and serve.

SERVES 6

SUPER-HOT SALSAS, MARINADES & PASTES

VERY HOT

HARISSA PASTE

This fiery paste is primarily associated with Tunisia, but it is also used in Algeria and Morocco. As well as a condiment, served in a small dish with a small spoon, this is used to add extra spice to meat, poultry, or vegetable casseroles, fish soups, or stewed red bell peppers with tomatoes.

⌁ INGREDIENTS ⌁

- 2 oz dried red chilies like African bird's eye or cayenne, soaked in hot water for 1 hour
- 2 garlic cloves, chopped
- 2 tsp coriander seeds
- 2 tsp cumin seeds
- 2 tsp caraway seeds
- pinch of salt
- 6 tbsp olive oil

1. Drain the chilies and put in a mortar, spice grinder, or small blender with the garlic, spices, and salt.

2. Mix to a paste, then stir in 3 tablespoons of the oil. Transfer to a small jar and pour the rest of the oil over the surface. Cover and keep in a cool, dark place, or the refrigerator, for 4–6 weeks.

RED & GREEN CURRY PASTE

VERY HOT

These classic Indonesian spice pastes are great for making slow-cooked curries. Simply blend all the ingredients together in a food processor.

⌒INGREDIENTS⌒

Green curry paste

- 6 medium green chilies, like Anaheim or jalapeño, deseeded and roughly chopped
- 2 stalks of lemongrass, outer leaves removed, chopped
- 2 tbsp roughly chopped cilantro leaves
- 2 tbsp roughly chopped Thai basil leaves
- 1 shallot, peeled and chopped
- 3 garlic cloves, peeled and minced
- 1 tsp shrimp paste
- 2 tsp ginger purée
- 4 kaffir lime leaves, chopped

⌒INGREDIENTS⌒

Red curry paste

- 6 medium red chilies, like pasilla or poblano, deseeded and chopped
- 2 red onions, peeled and chopped
- 4 cloves garlic, peeled and chopped
- 1 tsp ground kencur or 1-inch (2.5-cm) piece gingerroot, peeled and finely chopped
- 6 fl. oz coconut milk

GARLIC PEPPER JELLY

PREP TIME
10 mins
COOKING TIME
15 mins

This is a delicious relish to serve with roasts and cold meats—why not spice up the traditional Sunday lunch?

ᘓ INGREDIENTS ᘔ

- 4 lb sour apples
- 2 heads garlic (about 25 cloves total)
- 10 small chili peppers, like pequin or bird's eye
- 2½ pints water
- 2½ lb preserving sugar

1. Cut the apples into 1-inch chunks, but do not peel or core them. Separate and peel the garlic cloves and cut each in half lengthwise. Halve the peppers. Put the apples, garlic, and peppers into a preserving pan with the water and stew for about an hour, until the apples are reduced to a pulp. Tip into a jelly bag or thick cloth, and leave to drain overnight. Do not be tempted to speed up the flow of juice by squeezing the bag, as this will only make the juice cloudy.

2. Measure the juice into a clean pan with 10 ounces of sugar to every 20 fluid ounces liquid. Stir over a gentle heat until the sugar has dissolved. Boil rapidly for 10 minutes, until a little of the jelly sets when cooled on a plate, and wrinkles when you push it with your finger.

CHILI PEANUT DRESSING

MEDIUM SPICE

A variation on the traditional peanut dressing, this works well with Asian-style salads and noodle dishes.

⌁ INGREDIENTS ⌁

- 4 tbsp groundnut oil
- 6 oz unroasted, unsalted peanuts
- 1 tsp fresh lemongrass purée
- 2 cloves garlic, peeled and minced
- 2 shallots, peeled and finely chopped
- 1 medium red bird's eye chili, seeded and finely chopped

1. Heat the oil in a skillet and stir-fry the peanuts until golden. Remove immediately from the pan with a slotted spoon, reserving 2 tablespoons of the oil. Drain the nuts on paper towels and let cool. Grind coarsely in a food processor.

2. Mix the lemongrass purée, garlic, shallots, chili, and shrimp paste together.

3. Reheat the reserved oil, add the garlic and shallot mixture, and cook for 2 minutes, stirring frequently. Add the coconut milk, lime juice, sugar, soy sauce, ground peanuts, and water and cook over a low heat for 10 minutes, stirring frequently.

VERY HOT

INDIAN-STYLE EGGPLANT RELISH

Most Indian relishes contain a large quantity of oil and are very hot, and this is no exception. It is an excellent dish to add in small quantities to shrimp curries.

⊱ INGREDIENTS ⊰

- 1 lb firm young eggplants, cut into 1-inch chunks
- salt
- 1 tbsp cumin seeds
- 10 fl. oz groundnut oil
- 2 large onions, chopped
- 4 garlic cloves, peeled and minced
- 2-inch piece gingerroot, peeled and minced
- 1 tsp ground turmeric
- 2 tbsp light brown sugar
- 4 hot red bird's eye chilies, finely sliced
- 2 green habañero or Scotch bonnet chilies, finely sliced

1. Layer the eggplants in a colander, sprinkling each layer with salt. Leave for at least 1 hour. Rinse thoroughly under cold running water, then pat dry on paper towel.

2. Heat a large skillet over moderate heat, then add the cumin seeds and dry-fry them for 30 seconds, until fragrant and just starting to color. Tip onto a plate and leave to cool.

3. Heat the oil in the skillet. Add the eggplants and onion and cook for 3–4 minutes, then add the garlic, gingerroot, and turmeric and continue cooking for a further 2 minutes. Let cool slightly, then mix the sugar into the oil with 1 teaspoon of salt.

4. Pack the mixture into warmed jars, layering them with the sliced chilies. Press down firmly. Top up with oil, then seal.

MEDIUM SPICE

ONION AND CHILI SALSA

Broiling brings out a different aspect of chilies, as it does with onions and garlic. It mellows these ingredients and draws out their sweetness, giving this salsa a completely different character from those that are made raw.

❧ INGREDIENTS ❧

- ◆ 1 onion, unpeeled, cut in half
- ◆ 10 cloves garlic, whole, unpeeled
- ◆ 3 pequin or manzano chilies
- ◆ 1 green bell pepper, cut in half
- ◆ 1 large tomato, chopped
- ◆ sea salt, to taste
- ◆ juice of ½ lemon, or to taste

1. Broil the onion, garlic, chilies, and green pepper over medium heat, turning once, until charred on both sides. Remove from the heat and place in a paper bag to cool.

2. When cool enough to handle, remove the skins and stems, remove the seeds from the chilies, and chop. Combine all the ingredients in a bowl. Season with salt and lemon juice.

MANGO, PAPAYA, & CHILI RELISH

MEDIUM SPICE

Serve this relish as a side dish with rich barbecued foods, rice, and curries. The mango and papaya must be underripe.

INGREDIENTS

- 2 underripe green mangoes, peeled and thinly sliced
- 1 underripe green papaya, peeled and thinly sliced
- 1 red onion, slice thinly
- 2–3 perón rojo or manzano chilies, sliced thinly
- sugar, to taste
- sea salt, to taste

1. Serve the sliced mango and papaya sprinkled with half the chilies, the sugar, and salt. Sprinkle with additional chilies to taste.

PREP TIME
10 mins
COOKING TIME
15 mins

VERY HOT

CLASSIC JERK RUB

Use this recipe for classic, spicy jerk chicken.

⌘INGREDIENTS⌘

- 3 tbsp stemmed, deseeded, and chopped bird's eye or jacquin chilies
- 4 tsp allspice berries, crushed in a pestle and mortar or 1 tsp ground allspice
- 6 cloves garlic, peeled and minced
- 2 tbsp gingerroot, peeled and chopped
- 2 tbsp unrefined dark brown sugar
- 3 tbsp yellow mustard
- 1 tsp ground cinnamon
- hot pepper sauce, to taste
- 4 fl. oz olive oil
- 2 scallions, sliced
- 3 fl. oz cider vinegar
- 2 tbsp lime juice
- salt and pepper

1. Put the chili peppers in a blender or food processor and purée.

2. Add the allspice, garlic, gingerroot, sugar, mustard, cinnamon, hot pepper sauce, olive oil, scallions, vinegar, and lime juice and blend until the mixture forms a smooth paste.

3. Add salt and pepper to taste and blend again.

MILD SPICE

SPICED TOMATO CHUTNEY

Of all the recipes for chutneys, there must be more for tomato chutney than for any other. This is my favorite—rich and spicy.

↬ INGREDIENTS ↫

- 2 large red onions, chopped
- 4–6 large garlic cloves, chopped
- 9 oz cooking apples, cored and chopped (not peeled)
- 1 fresh red jalapeño chili, finely chopped
- 6 tbsp finely chopped gingerroot
- 3 tbsp ground cumin
- 2 tbsp dried oregano
- 2½ lb firm ripe tomatoes, cored and chopped
- 1 cup red wine vinegar
- 4 oz soft light brown sugar

1. Put all the ingredients in a nonreactive pan, bring to a boil, and simmer, stirring as necessary, until the chutney is thick. The chutney is ready when no liquid appears in the channel that is left when the spoon is drawn across the bottom of the pan. It will thicken further upon standing.

2. Prepare and fill sterilized jars, then seal with waxed paper disks and vinegar-proof lids. Let cool, label the jars, and store in a cool, dark, dry place for one month before eating. Keep for up to 1 year.

MILD SPICE

PREP TIME
5 mins
COOKING TIME
5 mins

ASIAN PESTO

Keep this in the refrigerator for when you don't have the energy to make a meal. Throw some salmon on the broiler, serve with a generous spoonful of pesto, and call it a night.

INGREDIENTS

- juice of 1 lime
- 1 oz Thai basil leaves
- 50 rau ram leaves
- 2 oz toasted unsalted cashews, ground (optional)
- 1 cayenne or bird's eye chili, deseeded and chopped
- 3 cloves garlic, peeled and minced
- 1 tsp gingerroot, peeled and shredded
- 5 tbsp vegetable or sunflower oil

1. Mix together all the ingredients and heat in a saucepan. Bring to a boil and simmer for 3 minutes.

2. Chill in the refrigerator before using.

SAMBAL OELEK

VERY HOT

This superhot sauce is great for adding to recipes. Use it sparingly with fishcakes or spring rolls.

INGREDIENTS

- 30 red bird's eye, habañero, or Scotch bonnet chilies
- 2 cloves garlic, peeled
- ¼ onion
- 2 tbsp sugar
- 2 tbsp lemon or lime juice
- 2–3 tbsp water

1. Combine all the ingredients in a blender and blend until a smooth paste forms. Transfer to a pan and cook for 10 minutes on a medium heat.

2. Cool and store in an airtight jar in the refrigerator for up to 2 weeks.

MEKONG CURRY PASTE

As with its neighbors Vietnam, Laos, Burma, and Thailand, Cambodia has its own version of fish sauce called *nguoc mam*, which is an integral part of the country's cuisine. Both the Mekong River and the sea produce a plentiful supply of fish and shellfish which are used to make curries with this paste.

INGREDIENTS

- 3 cloves garlic, peeled and chopped
- 1 large onion, peeled and chopped
- 1 stalk lemongrass, outer leaves removed and stem chopped
- 1-inch piece gingerroot, peeled and chopped
- 2 tsp coriander seeds
- 1 red japone or bird's eye chili, deseeded and chopped
- ½ tsp turmeric
- 2 tbsp peanut oil

1. Place all the ingredients in a food processor and blend to a paste, stopping periodically to push down the contents of the bowl as they spread up the sides.

PREP TIME
10 mins
COOKING TIME
15 mins

DEVILED TOMATO SAUCE

For depth of flavor and greater control, use mustard powder, as it only becomes fierce when mixed to a paste with water.

INGREDIENTS

- 1 tbsp butter
- 1 small onion, chopped
- 1 red Anaheim chili, deseeded and chopped
- 1–2 garlic cloves, crushed
- 1 small red bell pepper, deseeded and chopped
- 1–3 tsp mustard powder
- 1 tbsp all-purpose flour
- 8 oz tomatoes, peeled and chopped
- 1 tbsp tomato paste
- 4 tbsp stock or water
- 1–2 tsp Worcestershire sauce
- salt and freshly ground pepper

1. Melt the butter in a pan and gently sauté the onion, chili, and garlic for 3 minutes. Add the chopped pepper with the mustard powder and flour, and cook for a further 2 minutes.

2. Add the tomatoes, then blend the tomato paste with the stock or water, and add to the pan with the Worcestershire sauce. Bring to a boil, then cover and simmer for 10 minutes, stirring occasionally.

3. Add the seasoning to taste, stir well, and serve the sauce hot.

MEDIUM SPICE

GREEN TOMATILLO SAUCE

Tomatillos are a variety of green tomato with inflated papery skins. They have a bitter flavor with overtones of lemon. The bitterness is lost when the fruit is cooked. You can substitute green tomatoes if tomatillos are not available, but add a little lemon juice to recreate the lemony flavor.

⚞ INGREDIENTS ⚟

- 1 tbsp oil
- 1–2 garlic cloves, crushed
- 1–2 red serrano or cayenne chilies, chopped and deseeded
- 10 oz tomatillos, chopped
- 4 fl. oz vegetable stock
- 1–2 tsp clear honey
- salt and freshly ground pepper
- 2 tbsp chopped fresh cilantro
- 2 tbsp lime juice
- 1–1½ tbsp arrowroot

1. Heat the oil in a pan and gently sauté the garlic, chilies, and tomatillos for 5 minutes. Add the stock and honey, season to taste, then simmer for 10 minutes or until the tomatillos are soft and pulpy.

2. Rub through a fine-meshed sieve and return to the cleaned pan. Add the cilantro, blend the lime juice and arrowroot together, and stir into the pan. Cook, stirring, until the sauce thickens and clears. Adjust the seasoning and serve warm or cold.

GUACAMOLE

MEDIUM SPICE

An irresistible, fiery Mexican dip to enjoy with a glass of something cool on a summer's evening.

INGREDIENTS

- 2 large ripe avocados, halved and pitted
- 1 clove garlic
- 6 scallions, finely chopped
- 2 tomatoes, skinned, deseeded, and chopped
- 1 small green poblano or pequin chili, finely chopped
- 1 tbsp chopped fresh cilantro
- juice of 1 lime
- salt and freshly ground pepper

1. Using a teaspoon, scrape the avocado flesh into a bowl. Use a fork to beat it to a smooth purée.

2. Crush the garlic to a paste with a little salt and add to the bowl with all the other ingredients. Beat again until well mixed. Chill until required.

ADOBO SAUCE

VERY HOT

This Mexican sauce is fairly time-consuming to make, but it will keep for months in the refrigerator. If you can't get guajillos, replace with all ancho chilies.

❧ INGREDIENTS ❧

- 2 oz dried ancho chilies
- 1 ½ oz dried guajillos or rocoto chilies
- 8 cloves garlic, unpeeled
- ½-inch cinnamon stick
- 2 whole cloves
- 10 black peppercorns
- 2 large bay leaves, torn up
- large pinch cumin seeds
- ½ tsp dried oregano
- ½ tsp dried thyme
- 3 tbsp wine or cider vinegar
- 1–2 tsp salt

1. Toast the dried chilies for 2–3 minutes in a dry skillet, then soak in warm water for 15 minutes. Dry-fry the unpeeled garlic in a heavy skillet. Turn frequently. After 10–15 minutes, the garlic will be very soft and the blackened, blistered skins can be easily removed.

2. Grind the cinnamon, cloves, peppercorns, bay leaves, and cumin in a pestle and mortar or spice grinder. The aroma of freshly ground spices is incomparably superior to ready-ground spices.

3. Drain the chilies, and put them in a blender with the peeled garlic, herbs and spices, vinegar, and 2 tablespoons of water. Blend this mixture to a smooth paste for 5–10 minutes. You will need to stop every few seconds, and push the mixture down on to the blades. You may need to add another tablespoon of water.

Super-hot salsas, marinades, pastes & rubs **77**

VERY HOT

GARLIC,
CILANTRO & CHILI SAUCE

This sauce is made with three ingredients that are ubiquitous in Thai cuisine. Add extra chilies if you like things hot!

⊱INGREDIENTS⊰

- ½-oz fresh cilantro
- 4 cloves garlic, peeled and minced
- 1 medium red bird's eye chili, deseeded and finely chopped
- ¼ cup vegetable oil

1. Remove the leaves from the cilantro and chop coarsely. Chop the stalks finely. Mix with the chili and vegetable oil.

VERY HOT

HOT PEPPER AND LIME PASTE

This hot and flavorful paste, based on the Sudanese dish *shaata*, is made with mild chilies, paprika, and freshly squeezed lime juice. The paste is delicious added to stews, spicy soups, or Asian noodle dishes. It can also be a marinade for barbecued foods.

❧ INGREDIENTS ☙

- 1 tsp mild chili powder or ground ancho chilies
- 2 tsp paprika
- juice of ½ lime
- several generous pinches of salt

1. Stir all the ingredients together and mix well. Let stand for at least 10 minutes before serving, so the flavors can develop.

SESAME DIPPING SAUCE

This is a traditional Burmese recipe. Burmese cuisine does not use a large selection of spices: garlic, chilies, turmeric, and ginger are the most common seasonings.

INGREDIENTS

- 1 tbsp white sesame seeds
- 4 tbsp light soy sauce
- ¼ tsp ngapi (dried shrimp paste)
- 1 tbsp white wine vinegar
- ½ tsp sugar
- 1 small red bird's eye or serrano chili, deseeded, and chopped

1. Toast the sesame seeds in a dry, heavy skillet until just golden.

2. Remove immediately from the pan and mix with the soy sauce, shrimp paste, vinegar, and sugar, stirring until the sugar dissolves.

3. Serve in a small bowl, sprinkled with the chili.

FISH & SEAFOOD

MILD SPICE

LOBSTER IN CHILI SAUCE

This Asian-style dish is a good twist on the classic Singapore chili crab. Although a dry white is used in the cooking, a light, sweet accompanying wine will reduce the heat and complement the rich flavor of the lobster.

INGREDIENTS

- 2 x 2-lb cooked lobsters, split in half lengthwise
- 2 tbsp vegetable oil mixed with 1 tsp liquid achiote
- ¾ pint dry white wine
- 1 tsp salt
- ½ Anaheim chili pepper, finely chopped

SERVES 2

1. Remove and discard the gelatinous sac in the head of each lobster and the long intestinal vein attached to it. Chop off the tail section of each lobster at the point where it joins the body. Twist off the claws and smash the flat side of each claw with a large, heavy knife. Cut off and discard the small claws and antennae.

2. Heat the oil in a large skillet. Add the lobster bodies, tails, and large claws and fry them, stirring constantly until the shells turn pink. Transfer the lobsters to a large plate.

3. Add the wine to the skillet and bring it to the boil. Stir in the salt and chili pepper. Return the lobsters to the pan, coat them evenly in the liquid, and simmer for 10 minutes, basting them from time to time.

4. To serve, arrange the lobster pieces in a large, heated dish and spoon the sauce over them.

MEDIUM
SPICE

TUNA WITH MANGO SALSA

This recipe, using a mango salsa, would work well with swordfish or salmon. Beat the refried beans so that they are not too lumpy.

⌐INGREDIENTS⌐

- 1 tsp sunflower oil
- 3 tbsp white wine
- 15-oz can refried beans
- 4 x 5-oz tuna steaks
- salt and fresh ground pepper
- 1 small ripe mango, peeled, pitted, and finely chopped
- 4 shallots, peeled and chopped
- 1–2 green jalapeño chilies, deseeded and chopped
- 1–2 garlic cloves, peeled and minced
- 3 ripe but firm tomatoes, deseeded and chopped
- 2 tbsp chopped fresh cilantro
- flat-leaf parsley sprigs, to garnish
- rice and salad, to serve

1. Preheat the oven to 400°F (200°C). Lightly oil an oven-proof casserole dish with the sunflower oil. Place the wine and beans into the dish and heat through while preparing the remaining ingredients. Lightly rinse the tuna steaks, pat dry, season, and reserve. Stir together the mango, shallots, chilies, garlic, tomatoes, and cilantro.

2. Beat the refried beans in the dish until smooth, then place the tuna on top of the beans. Reduce the heat to 325°F (160°C). Spoon over the mango salsa, cover, and cook for 1 hour. Garnish with parsley sprigs and serve with rice and a salad.

SERVES 4

SPICY GARLIC SHRIMP

VERY HOT

The silky sweetness of coconut milk combines with fiery spices to make this shrimp dish a perfect dinner party recipe. Reduce the quantity of chili for a milder dish or simply remove the seeds, where most of the "heat" is found.

❧ INGREDIENTS ☙

- 10 oz uncooked shrimp, peeled and deveined
- 2 large zucchini, julienned
- 1 medium red bell pepper, julienned
- 3 bird's eye chilies, deseeded and chopped
- 2 medium tomatoes, chopped
- 2 tbsp olive oil
- 1 tsp fresh gingerroot, grated
- 4 garlic cloves, peeled and minced
- juice and zest of 1 medium lime
- 1 tsp ground coriander
- 1 tsp ground cumin
- 4 tbsp coconut milk
- 1 tbsp light soy sauce
- 8 oz dry egg noodles

1. Rinse the shrimp under running water and pat dry. Put in a shallow glass dish with the vegetables. Mix the oil, gingerroot, garlic, lime, spices, coconut milk, and soy sauce together, and pour over the ingredients. Stir to coat, cover, and marinate for 1 hour, turning occasionally.

2. Half-fill the base of the steamer with water and bring to the boil. Cover the base of the steamer top with dampened waxed paper and add the shrimp, vegetables, and marinade. Place over the steamer base, cover and steam for 10 minutes. Put the noodles into boiling water in the steamer base. Return the noodles and shrimp to the heat and cook for a further 5 minutes or until cooked.

3. Remove the steamer top and drain the noodles. Arrange on a plate and top with the shrimp mix.

SERVES 4

SHRIMP AND MARROW CURRY

MEDIUM SPICE

Using Mekong Curry Paste, this Cambodian recipe comes alive. Cambodian cuisine is often described as similar to the food of its Thai and Laotian neighbors but with a hint of Chinese stirred in for good measure. This curry can also be made with cubes of a firm white fish.

INGREDIENTS

- 2 tbsp peanut oil
- 1 quantity Mekong Curry Paste (page 73)
- 9 oz peeled, deseeded, 1-inch pieces of vegetable marrow
- 2 tbsp fish sauce
- 1 tbsp lemon juice
- 1 tsp unrefined dark brown sugar
- 1 tsp fresh lemongrass purée
- 10 fl. oz coconut milk
- 1 lb 2 oz large raw shrimp, peeled and deveined
- 1 red onion, finely chopped, to garnish
- 1 poblano chili, deseeded and finely chopped
- boiled rice, to serve

1. Heat the oil in a wok with a lid or a large skillet. Add the Mekong Curry Paste and fry over very low heat for 10 minutes or until softened and golden brown.

2. Add the marrow, fish sauce, lemon juice, sugar, lemongrass purée, and coconut milk. Cover the pan and simmer for 5 minutes.

3. Stir in the shrimp, uncover the pan, and cook for a further 5 minutes until the shrimp turn pink and the marrow is tender.

4. Garnish with chopped red onion and green chili. Serve with boiled rice.

SERVES 4

VERY
HOT

MIXED FISH CREOLE STYLE

This extra-hot fish dish is also known as *jambalaya*. Many different white fish fillets can be used, such as hoki, pollock, or cod. You could serve with white rice and a salad for a traditional main meal.

⌐ INGREDIENTS ⌐

- 2 tbsp oil
- 1 large onion, chopped
- 2 garlic cloves, peeled and minced
- 4–5 rocotilo or Scotch bonnet chili peppers, deseeded and chopped
- 2 celery sticks, chopped
- 1 red bell pepper, sliced
- 1 green bell pepper, sliced
- 2 tbsp tomato purée
- ½ pint fish or chicken stock
- 14-oz can chopped tomatoes
- 1 tsp Worcestershire sauce
- salt and pepper
- 8 oz white fish fillets
- 4 oz mackerel fillets
- 1 tbsp freshly chopped oregano
- 1 tbsp freshly chopped marjoram
- 4 oz shrimp

1. Heat the oil in a large saucepan and sauté the onion, garlic, chilies, and celery for 5 minutes, or until softened. Add the bell peppers and cook for a further 3 minutes.

2. Blend the tomato purée with a little water and stir into the saucepan with the stock, chopped tomatoes, Worcestershire sauce, and seasoning to taste. Bring to the boil, then reduce the heat and simmer for about 20 minutes.

3. Skin the fish fillets and discard any bones. Cut the fish into bite-sized pieces. Rinse and pat dry with paper towels.

4. Add the fish with the herbs and lime juice to the saucepan and simmer for a further 6 minutes. Add the shrimp and cook for a further 4 minutes, or until the fish is cooked.

SERVES 4

SQUID
WITH SAMBAL OELEK

MEDIUM SPICE

This Vietnamese recipe has a delicious texture, and the spicy sauce is highly addictive. Make sure you heat the peanut oil to the correct temperature before adding the squid so it cooks quickly and does not become tough and tasteless. Scoring the flesh in a criss-cross pattern beforehand will help.

INGREDIENTS

- 1 lb squid, cleaned and cut into small pieces
- 3 tbsp cornstarch
- ¼ tsp chili powder
- salt and freshly ground pepper
- peanut oil, for deep-frying
- 6 tbsp Sambal Oelek (see page 72)

1. Lightly score the pieces in a criss-cross pattern with a sharp knife. Season the cornstarch with the chili powder, a little salt, and plenty of freshly ground black pepper, and use to dust the squid until it is evenly covered.

2. Heat the peanut oil for deep-frying to 350°F (175°C) and fry the squid in two batches for about 2 minutes or until crisp. Drain on paper towels and serve with the Sambal Oelek.

SERVES 4

PREP TIME
10 mins

COOKING TIME
10 mins

MEDIUM SPICE

SHRIMP GREEN CURRY WITH BASIL

Thai basil, known as *bai jorapa*, sweet basil, or holy basil, has an aniseseed flavor quite different from the aromatic Italian or Greek basil. Bunches of it can be found in Chinese and Thai food stores.

⤢ INGREDIENTS ⤢

- 2 tbsp peanut oil
- 3 red shallots, peeled and sliced
- 7 oz pumpkin or butternut squash, peeled, deseeded, and cut into small pieces
- 1 zucchini, sliced
- 2 tbsp Green Curry Paste (page 59)
- 1 tbsp fish sauce
- 1 tbsp unrefined light brown sugar
- 14 fl. oz coconut milk
- 1 lb raw peeled shrimp
- 2 scallions, shredded, to garnish
- 1 green Anaheim chili, deseeded and finely sliced, to garnish
- Thai basil leaves, to garnish

1. Heat the peanut oil in a large skillet, add the shallots and pumpkin or butternut squash, and fry for 5 minutes, stirring occasionally.

2. Add the zucchini and 2 tablespoons of curry paste, and fry for a further 2 minutes. Any leftover curry paste can be stored in a small screwtop jar in the refrigerator.

3. Stir in the fish sauce, sugar, and coconut milk. Bring to a boil, lower the heat, and simmer for 15 minutes until the pumpkin or butternut squash is tender.

4. Add the shrimp and simmer for 2–3 minutes until they turn pink. Serve garnished with the scallions, green chili, and Thai basil leaves.

SERVES 4

SWORDFISH
WITH CASHEWS, VEGETABLES & RICE

MEDIUM SPICE

The swordfish in this dish has a wonderful texture—complemented by glorious Asian flavors.

INGREDIENTS

- 7 oz rice
- 1 lb swordfish, cleaned and prepared
- 2 oz cashew nuts
- 2 tbsp oil
- 1 bunch scallions, cut into 1-inch lengths
- 2 red bell peppers, deseeded and chopped
- 1 tsp freshly grated gingerroot
- 2 cloves garlic, chopped
- 5 oz jelly ear fungus (from a jar), washed
- 2 cayenne or serrano chilies
- 1 tbsp honey
- light soy sauce

1. Boil or steam the rice according to the package instructions.

2. Wash the fish, pat dry, and cut into bite-sized pieces.

3. Toast the cashews in a dry skillet.

4. Heat the oil in a wok and fry the fish. Add the scallions, reserving some for garnish, along with the peppers, and stir-fry briefly. Add a little water if necessary. Now add the ginger and garlic and finally the jelly ear fungus, honey, chili, and nuts. Fry for 1–2 minutes then add soy sauce to taste.

5. Serve in bowls garnished with the spring onions. Serve with the cooked rice.

SERVES 4

MEDIUM
SPICE

BABY CLAMS
WITH CHILI AND BASIL

This unusual mix of baby clams with chili works really well. It is a real lesson in seafood cooking, showing how not to be afraid to mix strong flavors with delicate fish.

INGREDIENTS

- 5 tbsp peanut or corn oil for frying
- 1 lb 6 oz fresh baby clams in their shells, cleaned well
- 1½ tbsp garlic, chopped
- 5 fresh red poblano chilies, sliced widthwise
- 2 tbsp Red Chili Paste (page 59)
- ¼ pint chicken stock
- 1 oz sweet basil leaves, plus extra to garnish

1. Heat the oil in a skillet or wok until quite hot, about 375°F (190°C). Add the clams and garlic, and cook until the clams open slightly, 2–3 minutes.

2. Add the fresh chilies, chili paste, and soy sauce, mix well, then pour in the chicken stock. Bring to a boil, cook for 2 minutes, stir in the basil, and serve immediately, garnished with the remaining basil and accompanied by rice.

SERVES 4

CRAB CAKES

MEDIUM SPICE

These are the perfect light Thai meal, but they also make a great snack to serve with cocktails. Try adding Green Curry Paste (page 59), or adding chopped lemongrass or grated lime rind to the mixture for a different spice sensation.

❧ INGREDIENTS ❧

- 12 oz crab meat
- 2 tsp Red Curry Paste (page 59)
- 1 tsp grated fresh gingerroot
- 2 tbsp chopped fresh cilantro
- ½ tsp fish sauce
- 2 tbsp all-purpose flour
- 1 egg, separated
- 1 tbsp cornstarch
- sunflower oil, for frying
- chili sauce, to serve

1. Put the crab meat, curry paste, ginger, cilantro, and fish sauce in a bowl and mix together well using a fork. Stir in the egg yolk, then sprinkle over the flour and mix well to combine. Shape the mixture into 16 small fish cakes.

2. Clean the mixer bowl and dry thoroughly, then whisk the egg white and cornstarch together with the wire whip on speed 8 until white and fluffy but not firm. Fold the egg whites gently into the crab mixture using a metal spoon, ensuring that it is well blended.

3. Heat about 1 tablespoon of oil in a non-stick pan. Fry the fish cakes in batches if necessary for 2–3 minutes on each side, until golden. Drain well on paper towel and serve hot, with chili sauce for dipping.

SERVES 4

PAD THAI

MEDIUM SPICE

Pad thai is probably Thailand's most famous noodle dish. Choose medium-sized shrimp rather than the very large ones. The peanuts should be natural, unsalted, and roasted in a dry, heavy skillet until golden. Take care not to burn them or they will have a bitter taste.

~ INGREDIENTS ~

- 12 oz medium flat rice noodles
- 1 quantity Garlic, Cilantro, and Chili Sauce (see page 78)
- 9 oz raw shrimp, peeled and coarsely chopped
- 4 shallots, peeled and sliced
- 1 tbsp sugar
- 4 large eggs, beaten
- 1 tbsp oyster sauce
- 2 tbsp nam pla (Thai fish sauce)
- juice of 1 lime
- 9 oz bean sprouts
- 4 scallions, shredded
- 1 cup unsalted, roasted peanuts, roughly chopped

1. Cook or soak the rice noodles according to the package instructions, then drain and set aside.

2. Heat the sauce in a pan. When hot, add the shrimp and shallots and stir-fry for 1 minute. Add the sugar and eggs and cook for a further 1 minute, stirring frequently.

3. Add the oyster sauce, fish sauce, lime juice, and drained noodles. Stir-fry for 2 minutes. Add the bean sprouts, scallions, and half the peanuts, and toss everything together over the heat until piping hot.

4. Spoon onto serving plates, sprinkle with the rest of the peanuts, and serve at once.

SERVES 4

MEAT & POULTRY

JERK MON'S CHICKEN

VERY HOT

This jerk dish is enriched by a super-hot rub that combines spices, brown sugar, and chili peppers and is applied to the chicken before cooking to make the finished dish sing.

INGREDIENTS

- 3 to 3½ lb chicken, jointed, or 6 large whole legs, or 4 large breast halves
- 1 quantity of Jerk Rub (page 67)

1. Separate the chicken legs and thighs. Cut breasts in half crosswise, leaving the wings attached. Gently lift the skin up from the chicken, exposing the meat, and spread some of the Jerk Rub underneath. Rub the remaining paste into the outside of the skin. Cover with plastic wrap and refrigerate for 2 hours.

2. To cook on a covered barbecue, place the coals on one side and the chicken on the other. Cover and cook for 40–50 minutes, then transfer it to the broiler and broil for 2–3 minutes on each side until the skin is dark brown and crusty. Serve with shredded cabbage and bell pepper salad, and kidney bean and rice salad.

SERVES 6

110 Spiced pork with onions, chilies & coconut

SPICED PORK
WITH ONIONS, CHILIES & COCONUT

MEDIUM SPICE

A pleasantly spiced oven pot roast with modern, fusion flavors, this is a great dinner party dish.

INGREDIENTS

- 2 tbsp sunflower or peanut oil
- 4 x 9-oz pork chops
- 2 large onions, quartered
- 1 tsp turmeric
- 2 bird's eye or habanero chilies, finely chopped
- 2 tsp fresh tamarind paste (optional)
- 3 to 4 lime leaves, finely chopped or finely grated zest of 2 limes
- 15 fl. oz milk
- 3 tbsp coconut cream
- salt and pepper

SERVES 4

1. Preheat the oven to 325°F (165°C). Heat the oil in an ovenproof casserole dish, then add the pork and brown quickly on all sides. Transfer to a plate.

2. Add the onions, chilies, spices, and lime leaves or zest to the pot and cook until the onions are lightly browned. Gradually add the milk, scraping up any bits from the bottom of the pan, then bury the pork back in among the onions.

3. Bring just to a boil, cover, and place in the oven for 2–2 ½ hours, until the meat is tender. Remove the meat from the ovenproof casserole and let stand for 10 minutes before carving.

4. Whisk the coconut cream into the spiced onions and milk, season, and heat gently until ready to serve. Carve the pork, and serve with the onion and coconut sauce spooned over.

PEPPERPOT

MEDIUM SPICE

This dish is said to come from Amerindian cuisine and is still eaten on many islands, including Tobago, St. Kitts, and Barbados. It seems a pepperpot is always simmering on the stove in the islands—some West Indians joke that the great-great-great grandmother started their pot going some decades ago.

⋞ INGREDIENTS ⋟

- 3 lb boiling chicken, trimmed of fat and cut into 12 pieces
- ½ lb fresh pig's foot
- 4 pints water
- 1½ tsp salt
- 3 lb boned pork or beef, cut into 2-inch cubes
- 6 tbsp cassareep sauce
- 1 large onion, sliced
- 1½ tbsp brown sugar
- 2 whole pequin or rocoto chilies
- 4 whole cloves
- 2-inch piece of cinnamon stick
- ¼ tbsp dried thyme
- 2½ tsp malt or distilled vinegar

SERVES 6

1. Put the chicken, pig's foot, and water into a large saucepan.

2. Add the salt and bring to a boil over low heat, skimming off any foam as it collects on the surface. Then reduce the heat, partially cover the pan, and simmer for about 1 hour or until the chicken is cooked.

3. Skim as much fat as possible from the surface of the soup. Stir in the pork or beef, cassareep, onion, brown sugar, chili peppers, cloves, cinnamon stick, and thyme. Bring to a boil over high heat, then lower the heat and simmer for 30 minutes, stirring occasionally, until the meat is cooked.

4. Remove the cloves, cinnamon stick, and chili peppers. Stir in the vinegar and taste, adjusting the seasoning if necessary.

114 Minced pork, shrimp & pineapple salad

MINCED PORK,
SHRIMP & PINEAPPLE SALAD

MEDIUM SPICE

This traditional Vietnamese recipe incorporates fresh chili—always a welcome addition to any salad—with spicy fish sauce.

INGREDIENTS

- 1 lb fresh lean pork, minced
- ½ tbsp water
- 8 oz cooked shrimp
- 2 tbsp lemon juice
- 2 tbsp nuoc mam (fish sauce)
- ½ tsp anchovy essence
- ½ tsp chili powder
- 1 tsp fresh red bird's eye chili pepper, finely sliced
- 2 tbsp scallions, cut into ½-inch sections
- 2 tbsp roasted peanuts
- 2 slices pineapple, chopped
- 2 tbsp gingerroot, finely sliced
- 1 tbsp fresh mint leaves, chopped
- 2 tbsp fresh cilantro leaves and stem, chopped
- 6 large lettuce leaves

1. Cook the pork in a wok over a medium heat with the water until the pork is cooked thoroughly but still tender and juicy. Remove from the heat.

2. Add the shrimp, lemon juice, nuoc mam, and dried and fresh chili and stir. Add the scallions, peanuts, pineapple, ginger, mint, and cilantro.

3. Serve on a bed of lettuce leaves.

SERVES 2

VERY
HOT

HOT AND STICKY SUMMERTIME CHICKEN

Here's an easy recipe for spatchcocked—split and broiled—chicken.

⌁ INGREDIENTS ⌁

- 3½–4½ lb whole chicken, prepared and flattened
- 1 x 12-oz can Dr. Pepper
- 10 cloves garlic, peeled and minced
- 3 whole habanero chilies
- 2 tbsp Louisiana hot sauce
- ½ cup grated onion
- 2 tbsp chopped fresh cilantro
- 2 tbsp chopped fresh parsley
- 2 tsp sea salt
- ½ cup clover honey
- 2 tbsp Dijon mustard
- 2 tbsp grated fresh gingerroot
- 1 tbsp grated orange zest
- 1 tbsp grated lime zest

1. Place the chicken in a resealable plastic bag. Combine the next 8 ingredients in a bowl. Pour over the chicken and seal the bag. Refrigerate for a minimum of 3 hours, or overnight.

2. In a small bowl, combine the final 5 ingredients. Preheat the barbecue to medium heat. Place the bird on the rack, bone-side down. Discard the bag and the marinade. Cook the chicken for approximately 15–20 minutes on each side. When its internal temperature reaches 165°F (73°C), start to brush on the glaze. Continue brushing on the glaze until it is used up and the meat reaches 170°F (76°C). Remove the chicken from the broiler and let sit for 10 minutes before serving.

SERVES 8

VERY HOT

RENDANG SAPI
INDONESIAN RED BEEF CURRY

Long, slow cooking means the beef in this dish becomes deliciously tender and full of flavor as it absorbs the spices and coconut milk. Quite dry, this is a popular dish in Padang, western Sumatra.

⚜ INGREDIENTS ⚜

- 3 tbsp vegetable oil
- 1 quantity Red Curry Paste (see page 59)
- 1 lb 9 oz rump steak, cubed
- 1 tsp turmeric
- 1 tbsp ground coriander
- 6 curry leaves
- 5 fl. oz coconut milk
- 1 tbsp tamarind pulp, infused in 5 fl. oz boiling water for 10 minutes, then strained
- 2 tsp palm sugar or unrefined dark brown sugar
- salt

1. Heat the vegetable oil in a large heavy saucepan, add the curry paste, and cook over a low heat for 5 minutes.

2. Add the steak, turmeric, ground coriander, and curry leaves. Stir well and cook gently for a further 10 minutes.

3. Stir in the coconut milk and strained tamarind liquid and cook, covered, over the lowest possible heat for 1 hour, then uncover and cook for a further 30 minutes until the meat is tender and the sauce has reduced and thickened.

4. Stir in the sugar and add salt to season, if necessary.

SERVES 4

FEIJOADA

Feijoada, a spicy stew of black beans and pork, is the ceremonial dish of Brazil. Traditionally it is made with various parts of the pig, such as snout, ears, tail, and feet. This version uses pork loin and linguica, a garlicky Portuguese sausage. Serve Feijoada with rice, greens, and orange slices.

⌘ INGREDIENTS ⌘

- 2 cups dry black beans, picked over and soaked overnight
- 4 tbsp vegetable oil
- 3 dried de arbol or manzano chilies, whole
- 8 cloves garlic, peeled and minced
- 2 lb pork loin, cubed
- 1 large onion, chopped
- 1 pound linguica, cut into ¼-inch slices
- 3 jalapeño chilies, deseeded and minced
- about 2 tsp salt

SERVES 8-10

1. Drain the beans, put them in a stockpot and add enough water to cover by 2 inches. Bring to a boil, reduce heat and simmer.

2. Heat 1 tablespoon of the oil in a small skillet and sauté the chilies de arbol and half the minced garlic for 1–2 minutes, until the garlic just starts to brown. Add to the beans. Heat another 1 tablespoon oil in large skillet and sauté the onion and remaining half of the minced garlic for 5 minutes, then add to the beans.

3. Add the linguica to the beans. Return the stew to a boil, reduce heat and simmer. When beans have simmered for 1 hour, add the jalapeños. Continue simmering until the beans are tender, a total of 1 ½–2 hours. Add salt to taste.

122 Roasted spareribs with lemongrass and chili

MEDIUM SPICE

SPARERIBS
WITH LEMONGRASS AND CHILI

These spareribs are perfect for a cookout or to serve to dinner guests. They are zesty, savory, herby, peppery, and so full of flavor.

⌐INGREDIENTS⌐

- 12 pork spareribs
- 2 tbsp clear honey
- 1 tsp five-spice powder
- 2 cloves garlic, finely chopped
- 3 tbsp dry sherry or rice wine
- 3 tbsp fish sauce or 3 tbsp light soy sauce mixed with 1 tsp anchovy extract
- 2 stalks fresh lemongrass, sliced thinly, or grated peel of 1 lemon
- 2 fresh cayenne chili peppers, finely chopped

1. Wash and dry the spareribs and place them in a large bowl.

2. In another bowl, combine the honey, five-spice powder, garlic, dry sherry, fish or soy sauce, lemongrass, and chili. Mix well. Spread the mixture over the spareribs and leave to marinate for 4 hours.

3. The ribs can be cooked over a barbecue, turning frequently; or baked in the oven at 375°F (190°C); or broiled under a moderately hot broiler. Baste the ribs with the marinade during cooking.

SERVES 4

PREP TIME
30 mins
COOKING TIME
2½ hours

PORK AND CHORIZO CHILI

This is a very hearty chili with bold flavors. Using a combination of 2 dried California chilies, 2 dried New Mexico chilies, and 2 dried chilies negros, it is hot but not fiery. Vary the chilies to suit your taste.

INGREDIENTS

- 6 large dried chilies, deseeded and chopped
- 3 tbsp vegetable oil
- 2 lb pork, cubed
- 1½ medium onions, chopped
- 1 stalk celery, finely chopped
- ½ green bell pepper, chopped
- 4 cloves garlic, peeled and minced
- 2 beef bouillon cubes
- 2 tsp ground cumin
- 2 tsp dried oregano
- 1 tsp ground coriander
- pinch dried sage
- ½ tsp sugar
- 8 oz chorizo sausage (unsmoked)
- 2 tbsp masa harina flour
- 1–2 tsp salt

1. Place chilies in a small heatproof bowl, add ½ pint water, and stir to be sure all pieces are covered. Let soak for 30 minutes.

2. Meanwhile, heat 1 tablespoon of the oil in a skillet and cook the pork, stirring occasionally, until lightly browned. Remove the meat with a slotted spoon and discard the greasy cooking liquids. Heat the remaining 2 tablespoons of oil in the skillet and sauté the onion, celery, bell pepper, and garlic for 5 minutes.

3. Put the pork and vegetables in a large saucepan and add water to cover. Bring to a boil, reduce heat, and simmer. Dissolve the boullion cubes in ½ pint of hot water and add to the chili. Add the cumin, oregano, coriander, sage, and sugar.

4. Put the dried chilies and their soaking liquid in a blender or food processor. Purée until smooth. Strain to remove the seeds and bits of skin and discard the solids. Add the sauce to the chili.

5. After the chili has cooked for about 1 hour, crumble the chorizo into a hot skillet and fry for 1–8 minutes, until all the fat has rendered out. Remove from the heat and tilt the pan to drain the fat. With a slotted spoon, remove the chorizo and add to the chili. Discard the fat.

6. Continue simmering until the pork is tender, at least 1 ½ hours, adding water if needed. When the chili is ready, dissolve the masa harina in 2 fluid ounces of cold water to make a paste. Add to the chili, and stir well. Add salt, taste, and adjust the seasonings.

SERVES 4

VERY HOT

EYE-POPPING CHILI WITH CORN

This chili starts with a hot bottle of salsa and gets hotter with New Mexico chili powder. The corn adds a pleasing sweetness and a bit of crunch. If you have fresh corn, hold it over the pot as you cut the corn off the cob so that the milky liquid drips into the chili. Otherwise, frozen corn is fine.

INGREDIENTS

- 3 tbsp vegetable oil
- 12 fl. oz bottled hot salsa
- 2 beef bouillon cubes
- 1 medium onion, chopped
- 2 lb beef, cubed or coarsely ground
- 2 tbsp hot New Mexico chili powder
- 2 tbsp chili powder
- 1 tsp ground cumin
- 1 tsp dried oregano
- 1 tsp garlic powder
- 1 tsp celery salt
- 1 cup corn, about 2 ears
- 1 tsp salt

1. Heat 1 tablespoon of the oil in a large saucepan. When the oil is sizzling hot, add the salsa and fry for 5 minutes. Dissolve the bouillon cubes in ½ pint of boiling water and add it to the salsa with 1 more pint of water.

2. Heat 1 tablespoon of the oil in a skillet and sauté the onion for 5 minutes. Add the onion to the salsa. Heat the remaining oil and cook the beef until lightly browned. Add to the salsa with the remaining ingredients, except the corn and salt. Simmer for 1 hour. Add the corn and simmer for 30 minutes. Add salt, taste, and adjust seasonings.

SERVES 4–6

BARBECUED KOREAN LAMB

Kochujang is a Korean chili paste used for glazing meat or adding to stir-fries, stews, and dips. It can be bought from Asian stores but if you cannot find it, use whatever chili paste you have available—or make your own with the recipe on page 59.

⋐INGREDIENTS⋑

- 2 tsp kochujang chili paste
- 2 tbsp rice vinegar
- 4 tbsp Japanese soy sauce
- 3 tbsp mirin
- 1 tsp sesame oil
- 12 lamb cutlets
- ½ cucumber, grated
- 1 tsp salt
- 3-inch piece of white radish, grated

SERVES 4

1. Mix together the chili paste, rice vinegar, Japanese soy sauce, mirin, and sesame oil.

2. Lay the lamb cutlets in a single layer in a shallow dish and spoon the marinade over them. Cover and leave to marinate overnight in a cool place.

3. To make the pickle, place the grated cucumber in a colander set on a large plate to catch the drips, sprinkle with the salt and leave for 30 minutes. Drain, rinse, and pat dry with a paper towel. Mix with the grated radish.

4. Broil or barbecue the lamb cutlets for 5–6 minutes, or until cooked to your liking, basting or brushing with any marinade left in the dish.

5. Serve with the cucumber pickle.

130 Chicken tandoori

CHICKEN TANDOORI

VERY HOT

This Indian dish is traditionally baked in a very hot clay tandoor oven, heated with charcoal. Barbecuing your chicken tandoori will create a similar smoky flavour and the marinade can be used to coat any meat or seafood.

INGREDIENTS

- 1½ tbsp coriander seeds
- 1½ tbsp cumin seeds
- 1 red bird's eye chili, deseeded
- 2 large cloves garlic
- 2-inch piece gingerroot
- 2 tbsp lemon juice
- 1 tsp garam masala
- 5 fl. oz low-fat plain yogurt
- few drops of red food coloring
- salt and freshly ground pepper
- 4 x 5-oz skinless, boneless chicken breasts
- lime wedges, to garnish

1. Dry-fry the coriander and cumin seeds for 3–4 minutes, stirring frequently and taking care not to burn the spices. Remove, then grind in a pestle and mortar.

2. In a blender, combine the chili, garlic, and gingerroot. Stir in the ground spices, then the lemon juice, and mix to a paste. Add the garam masala, the yogurt, and a few drops of food coloring to give a good red color, then season.

3. Rinse the chicken and pat dry. Make three slashes across each breast and place in a shallow dish. Pour over the tandoori paste, cover, and leave to marinate for at least 6 hours or overnight.

4. Preheat the broiler, or light the barbecue 20 minutes before cooking. Drain the chicken and cook for 20–25 minutes, or until the juices run clear. Serve garnished with lime wedges.

SERVES 4

132 Spicy basque beans with ham

VERY HOT

SPICY BASQUE BEANS WITH HAM

These beans might be served as a side dish at a Basque barbecue, but they can also be eaten as a light main dish.

⌐INGREDIENTS⌐

- 1 or 2 ham hocks
- 2 bay leaves
- 2 tbsp vegetable oil
- 1 large onion, chopped
- 4 cloves garlic, peeled and minced
- 1 stalk celery, finely chopped
- 14 oz red beans, picked over and soaked overnight
- 2 carrots, peeled and finely chopped
- 8-oz can tomato sauce
- 1 large or 2 small tomatoes, chopped
- 2–3 jalapeño or serrano chilies
- 1 tbsp chili powder
- ½ tsp ground cumin
- 15-oz can garbanzo beans
- 2–3 tsp salt

SERVES 6

1. Put the ham hocks and bay leaves in a large saucepan and add enough water to cover by 2 inches. Bring to a boil, and simmer for 30 minutes. While the ham hocks are simmering, cook the vegetables. Heat the oil in a large skillet and sauté the onion, garlic, and celery for 5 minutes. Drain the red beans.

2. Add the sautéed vegetables and red beans to the ham hocks. Bring to a boil, reduce heat, and simmer for 30 minutes. Remove the ham hocks and let cool for about 15 minutes. Meanwhile, add the remaining ingredients, except the garbanzo beans.

3. When the ham hocks are cool enough to handle, shred the meat and add it to the beans.

4. Cook the beans until they are tender, about 1 ½ hours. Add the garbanzo beans. Taste and adjust seasonings. Serve.

VEGETABLES

SPICY CABBAGE SZECHWAN STYLE

MEDIUM SPICE

This recipe is easy but it takes a lot of preparation and standing before serving, so allow plenty of time for the chili peppers to work their magic.

⌜INGREDIENTS⌟

- 1 lb white cabbage
- 2 tsp salt
- 3–4 dried ancho chili peppers, soaked and finely chopped
- 3 scallions, finely chopped
- 2 tbsp sesame seed oil
- 2 tbsp sugar
- 2 fl. oz water
- 2 tbsp vinegar

1. Discard the outer tough leaves of the cabbage and cut the tender heart into thin slices. Sprinkle with salt and let stand for 3–4 hours. Pour off the excess water and dry thoroughly. Place in a bowl or deep dish.

2. Heat the sesame seed oil in a pan until very hot. Add the finely chopped chilies and scallions. Stir for a few seconds and then add the sugar and water. Continue stirring to dissolve the sugar. Add the vinegar and bring the mixture to a boil. Remove the pan from the heat and allow the sauce to cool, then pour it over the cabbage. Cover the bowl or plate and let stand for 3–4 hours before serving.

SERVES 4

138 Gado-Gado with chili and peanut dressing

GADO-GADO WITH CHILI AND PEANUT DRESSING

MILD SPICE

This is an Indonesian mixed vegetable salad. Vegetables that cannot be eaten raw would usually be steamed to retain all their texture and flavor, but they could be blanched or boiled in a saucepan of water if preferred.

⚞ INGREDIENTS ⚟

- 1 medium carrot, peeled and thinly sliced
- 1 large potato, peeled and diced
- 4 oz green beans, cut into 1-inch lengths
- 4 oz bean sprouts, rinsed
- 5 oz mooli (white radish), peeled and cut into matchsticks
- 1 slice pineapple, cut into small chunks
- 4 oz Chinese cabbage, shredded
- 2 oz white cabbage, shredded
- 1 quantity Chili Peanut Dressing (page 61)
- 2 hard-boiled eggs, quartered or sliced, to garnish
- 4 oz cucumber, sliced or chopped, to garnish

1. Steam or boil the carrot and potato until tender. Drain and cool under cold water. Steam or blanch the green beans and bean sprouts for 1 minute. Drain and refresh under cold water.

2. Place the carrot, potato, beans, bean sprouts, mooli, and pineapple in a bowl and toss together.

3. Arrange the Chinese cabbage and white cabbage in a serving bowl and arrange the vegetables and pineapple in the center.

4. Dilute the dressing with extra warm water if necessary. Cool and spoon over the salad. Garnish with the hard-boiled eggs and cucumber. Serve right away.

SERVES 4

SPICED POTATO CAKES

MEDIUM SPICE

These tasty fried potato cakes come from Algeria. The spicy mashed potato mixture is also good served simply as it is.

❧ INGREDIENTS ❧

- 2 lb mashed potato
- 1 tbsp paprika pepper
- 2 tsp ground cumin
- good pinch of cayenne pepper
- 1 bunch of cilantro, chopped
- 3 eggs, beaten
- salt and pepper
- oil for frying

1. In a large bowl, mix the potato with the spices, cilantro, eggs, and seasoning. With floured hands, form the mixture into round flat cakes. Cover and chill for 30 minutes.

2. Heat a shallow layer of oil in a skillet, add the cakes in batches and fry until crisp and brown on both sides. Transfer to paper towels to drain. Serve hot.

SERVES 4–6

OKRA AND BEAN CURRY

VERY HOT

This sizzling vegetarian curry is not for the faint hearted. Luckily the inclusion of yogurt balances the heat!

INGREDIENTS

- 2 tbsp sunflower oil
- 1 large onion, sliced
- 2 garlic cloves, peeled and minced
- 4 jalapeno or green fresno chilies, deseeded and sliced
- 1 tsp ground coriander
- 1 tsp ground cumin
- 5 cloves, ground
- 8 green cardamom pods
- 1 tsp turmeric
- 1 tsp fenugreek seeds, lightly bruised
- ¾ pint vegetable stock
- 1 lb okra, trimmed
- 14-oz can pinto or kidney beans
- 4 tbsp plain yogurt
- 2 tbsp freshly chopped cilantro
- 1 oz toasted flaked almonds

1. Heat the oil in a pan and sauté the onion, garlic, and chilies for 5 minutes. Add the spices and sauté for a further 3 minutes. Stir in the stock and bring to a boil. Cover the pan, reduce the heat, and simmer for 10 minutes.

2. Prick the okra a few times with a fork and add to the pan with the rinsed beans. Cook gently for 8–10 minutes, or until the okra is tender. Stir in the yogurt and cilantro, and heat through for a further minute. Serve sprinkled with the almonds.

SERVES 4

144 Spicy potato curry with cardamom

MEDIUM SPICE

POTATO CURRY
WITH CARDAMOM

Widely known as the "queen of spices," cardamom is used in a variety of savory Indian dishes. In this dish, it complements the chili for a sophisticated spice sensation.

❦ INGREDIENTS ❧

- 1 tsp cumin seeds
- 1 tsp whole coriansder
- 1 tsp fenugreek seeds
- 5 cloves
- 6 cardamom pods
- 2 tbsp sunflower oil
- 1 large onion, sliced
- 2 garlic cloves, peeled and minced
- 4 red jalapeño chilies, deseeded and chopped
- 1½ lb potatoes, cubed
- 1 pint vegetable stock
- 1 red bell pepper, skinned, deseeded, and sliced
- 2 tbsp freshly chopped cilantro

1. Put the whole spices in a pestle and mortar or food processor and grind to a powder.

2. Heat the oil in a large pan and sauté the onion, garlic, and chilies for 5 minutes, or until softened. Add the ground spices and cook gently for a further 3 minutes, stirring occasionally.

3. Add the potatoes with the stock and bring to a boil. Cover the pan, reduce the heat, and simmer for 15 minutes, or until the potatoes are tender.

4. Add the sliced red bell pepper and cook for a further 5 minutes. Stir in the freshly chopped cilantro and serve immediately.

SERVES 4–6

MILD SPICE

BLACK BEAN
AND MANY PEPPER CHILI

This black bean chili, rich with sweet and spicy peppers, is delicious on its own in a bowl topped with sour cream, crisp tortilla chips, chopped onions, and grated cheese. It is also good as a sauce for most barbecued dishes and, thinned with broth, it makes a hearty soup.

⌒ INGREDIENTS ⌒

- 14 oz black beans
- 3 pints water
- 1¼ pint broth
- 2 mild ancho chilies, sliced
- 2 tbsp olive oil
- 2 red bell peppers, diced
- ½ green bell pepper, diced
- 1 onion, chopped
- ½ carrot, diced
- 8 cloves garlic, chopped
- 2 tsp mild chili powder
- 1 tbsp cumin
- 1 tsp oregano
- 1 tbsp paprika
- 14 oz tomatoes, chopped
- 1 red or green chili, such as Anaheim, chopped
- 1 oz chopped fresh cilantro

1. Put the beans and water in a saucepan and bring to a boil. Reduce the heat and cook until the beans are nearly tender, then add the broth and dried chilies, and continue to cook, adding more liquid if needed.

2. Pour the olive oil into a skillet and sauté the bell peppers, onion, carrot, and half the garlic, until softened. Sprinkle with chili powder, cumin, oregano, and paprika, and add the tomatoes. Cook for a few moments, then add to the simmering and almost-tender beans along with the remaining garlic and half the cilantro.

3. Continue to cook until the beans are very tender and the sauce is rich and dark. Add the fresh chili to taste. Serve sprinkled with the remaining cilantro.

SERVES 6

148 Saffron rice and almond salad

SAFFRON RICE AND ALMOND SALAD

MEDIUM SPICE

A lovely summer salad, served with raw shredded chilies. Be aware that if this salad is kept sitting around for too long the almonds will lose their crunch.

⚞INGREDIENTS⚟

- 1 cup long-grain rice
- 1 pint water
- good pinch salt
- ½ tsp saffron threads infused for ½ hour in 2 tbsp hot water
- ½ tsp English mustard
- 1 tbsp wine vinegar
- 3 tbsp olive oil
- 1 tsp sugar
- 3–4 oz blanched almonds
- 2 oz raisins
- 1–2 fresh datil chilies, seeded, rinsed, and sliced thin

1. Put the rice, water, salt, and saffron infusion in a saucepan, bring to a boil, and simmer, covered, until the water has been absorbed and the rice is just tender, for about 20–25 minutes. Take off the heat.

2. Combine the mustard, vinegar, oil, and sugar and stir into the hot rice. Chill.

3. Just before serving, toast the almonds under the broiler or in a moderate oven, shaking the pan from time to time, until lightly browned. Stir into the chilled rice with the raisins and chilies, and serve immediately.

SERVES 6

TABBOULEH WITH CHILIES

MILD SPICE

Tabbouleh comes from the Latin word *tabbûle*—which literally means "a little spicy." This version uses green chilies for that extra flavor. Serves as a main dish for two or a side dish as part of a mezze.

❧ INGREDIENTS ❧

- 4 oz bulgur
- 1 small onion, finely chopped
- 4 tbsp lemon juice
- 1 tsp salt
- 1–2 fresh green Anaheim chilies, deseeded and thinly sliced
- generous handful fresh mint leaves, coarsely chopped
- 4 tbsp olive oil
- lettuce leaves (optional)
- Salsa (page 65), to serve

1. Cover the bulgur with cold water and leave to soak for 15 minutes, then drain in a fine sieve or a colander lined with a dish towel.

2. Mix in the onion, lemon juice, salt, and chilies, and combine well. Chill.

3. To serve, stir in the mint and oil, and if you like, pile onto a bed of lettuce leaves. Serve with Tomato Salsa on top.

SERVES 4

PREP TIME
10 mins
COOKING TIME
45 mins

DAL DELUXE

A mainstay of Nepali, Indian, Pakistani, and Bangladeshi cuisine, dal is a popular vegetarian dish.

⊱ INGREDIENTS ⊰

- 2 tbsp ghee or oil
- 2 cloves garlic, minced
- 1 large onion, chopped
- 2 fresh green habanero chilies, deseeded and finely chopped
- 1 tsp ground turmeric
- 1 tbsp ground coriander
- ½ tsp ground cumin
- 6 oz orange split lentils, washed
- 1 tbsp tomato paste
- 2 tbsp tomato ketchup
- 1 pint chicken or vegetable broth
- salt, pepper, and sugar to taste

1. Heat the oil and fry the garlic, onion, chilies, and spices until lightly browned.

2. Add the lentils, tomato purée, and ketchup, and stir until well mixed.

3. Add broth and bring to the boil. Season.

4. Turn down the heat and simmer, stirring occasionally, for 35–45 minutes, until the lentils start to fall apart.

5. Just before serving, add seasoning.

SERVES 4-6

PEPPER AND BLACK BEAN RICE

VERY HOT

Black beans and rice are such a classic combination, especially in Caribbean or Creole cooking. There are probably dozens of ways to make this dish; this is an easy recipe that cooks up quickly and tastes great.

INGREDIENTS

- 8 oz dried black beans
- 40 fl. oz fresh water
- 1 bay leaf
- ½ cubanelle or poblano chili
- 4 tbsp olive oil, plus extra for frying
- 1 medium white onion, finely chopped
- 1 cubanelle or poblano chili, deseeded and choppped
- 2 garlic cloves, chopped
- ½ tsp dried oregano
- 16 oz white long-grain rice
- salt, to season
- 4 tbsp olive oil, plus extra for frying
- white vinegar, to season

SERVES 4

1. Soak the beans in water overnight. Drain.

2. The following day, combine the fresh water, beans, bay leaf, and the half pepper in a large saucepan and bring to a full boil. Reduce the heat and simmer, covered, until the beans are tender. Strain, and remove the pepper, reserving the cooking liquid.

3. Coat the bottom of a large saucepan with olive oil, and cook the onion, the rest of the diced chili pepper, chopped garlic, and oregano for about 4 minutes or until translucent.

4. Add the rice, beans, reserved cooking liquid, and salt, and bring to a boil. Reduce the heat and cook, covered until the rice is soft.

5. Season with vinegar to taste, and let it stand for at least 1 hour before serving.

SIZZLING
PASTA & RICE

PEARL RICE BALLS

MILD SPICE

Short-grain or sushi rice can be used for the recipe but soak it in a bowl of cold water for 2 hours before use to get rid of excess starch. Cook the rice balls in a bamboo or metal steamer adding chicken broth to the pan below for extra flavor.

INGREDIENTS

- 6 oz short-grain rice
- 8 oz ground pork
- 8 oz ground chicken
- 4 scallions, finely chopped
- 1 tsp fresh ginger purée
- 8 oz water chestnuts, finely chopped
- 1 tsp granulated sugar
- 3 tbsp dark soy sauce
- 1 tbsp tomato ketchup
- 1 red bird's eye chili, deseeded and chopped very finely
- 3 tbsp chopped cilantro leaves
- 2 tbsp almonds, finely chopped
- 1 egg, beaten
- chicken broth, for steaming

1. Put the rice in a bowl, cover with cold water, and leave to soak for 2 hours. Drain the rice and spread out on a large plate to dry.

2. In a bowl, mix together the pork, chicken, scallions, ginger puree, water chestnuts, sugar, dark soy sauce, tomato ketchup, red chili, cilantro, and almonds. Stir in the beaten egg, mixing well.

3. With damp hands, form the mixture into 24 walnut-sized balls and roll in the rice to coat. Place the balls in a lightly greased steamer.

4. Bring a pan of chicken broth to a boil and steam the rice balls for 20–25 minutes or until the rice and meat are cooked.

MAKES 24

160 Chili rice burgers

CHILI RICE BURGERS

These burgers can be grilled on the barbecue, but it is a good idea to put them in a broil basket to make it easier to turn them over.

INGREDIENTS

- 3 tbsp olive oil
- 2 cloves garlic, peeled and minced
- 4 japone or de arbol chilies, deseeded and chopped
- 2 oz short-grain rice
- 1 large carrot, shredded
- 2 tbsp tomato paste mixed with 2 tbsp water
- 1¼ pint vegetable broth
- 1–2 tbsp sea salt and freshly ground pepper, to taste
- 8-oz can red beans, drained
- 2 oz corn kernels
- 2 tbsp chopped cilantro
- 6 buns, lightly toasted
- Mango, Papaya & Chili Relish (page 66), to serve

SERVES 6

1. Heat 2 tablespoons oil in a skillet and sauté the garlic and chili for 5 minutes. Stir in the rice and cook for 3 minutes. Stir in the carrot.

2. Add the tomato paste mixture, vegetable broth, salt, and pepper to the skillet. Bring to a boil. Simmer for 20 minutes, until the rice is cooked.

3. Add the red beans and corn. Cook for another 5 minutes or until the mixture is very stiff and will stick together. Stir in the cilantro and remove from the heat. Let cool.

4. When the mixture is cool enough to handle, wet your hands and shape the mixture into 6 burgers. Cover and refrigerate for at least 30 minutes.

5. Brush the burgers with olive oil and broil over medium heat for 4–5 minutes, turn carefully, and cook another 3–4 minutes or until heated through. To serve, place the burgers on buns and top with Mango, Papaya & Chili Relish.

PASTA
WITH HOT PEPPER
SAUCE & BLACK OLIVES

MEDIUM SPICE

This Italian-inspired recipe can change to suit your mood—alter the number of chilies according to how hot they are and how spicy you want the sauce to be.

⚜ INGREDIENTS ⚜

- 5–6 fl. oz extra-virgin olive oil
- 3–6 pasilla chilies, chopped
- 14-oz can tomatoes, chopped
- salt and pepper to taste
- pinch sugar
- 10 cloves garlic, chopped or minced with a sprinkling of salt
- 12 oz spaghetti
- 3–4 tbsp tapenade

1. Place the olive oil and chilies in a saucepan and heat gently, allowing the peppers to cook but not fry. Cook over medium-low heat for 10–15 minutes; they will turn in color and lightly stew.

2. Add the tomatoes, salt, pepper, sugar, and about half the garlic. Continue to simmer for about 30 minutes or until the mixture is a thickened, sauce-like purée. Add the remaining garlic.

3. Cook the pasta in boiling salted water until al dente (tender, but still firm to the bite), then drain. Toss the hot, drained pasta with the hot spicy sauce, and serve immediately, with a spoonful of tapenade over each portion.

SERVES 4

164 Chili bean risotto

PREP TIME
10 mins
COOKING TIME
40 mins

VERY
HOT

CHILI BEAN RISOTTO

Packed full of the flavors of Mexico, this tasty risotto makes a substantial main meal served on its own.

INGREDIENTS

- 1½ pints vegetable broth
- 2 tbsp vegetable oil
- 1 large onion, finely chopped
- 4 oz button mushrooms
- 1 garlic clove, minced
- 2 pequin chilies, deseeded and finely chopped
- 2 green bell peppers, deseeded and diced
- 14 oz arborio rice
- 1 tsp ground cumin
- 1 tsp chili powder
- salt and ground pepper
- 14-oz can red beans, drained and rinsed
- 12-oz can corn, drained and rinsed
- 4 medium tomatoes, peeled, deseeded, and chopped, to serve

1. Pour the broth into a saucepan and bring to a gentle simmer.

2. Heat the oil in a large saucepan and fry the onion, mushrooms, garlic, chili, and green peppers for 4–5 minutes until softened. Stir in the rice and cook, stirring, until the rice is coated in the vegetable mixture.

3. Add a ladleful of broth and cook gently, stirring, until absorbed. Continue adding the stock ladle-by-ladle until half the stock is used. Stir in the spices, seasoning, and red beans.

4. When the risotto becomes thick, but not sticky (about 25 minutes), stir in the corn and tomatoes. Mix well, adjust seasoning if necessary, and serve.

SERVES 4

166 Char kway teow fried rice noodles

MEDIUM SPICE

CHAR KWAY TEOW
FRIED RICE NOODLES

Kway teow are rice noodles, also known as rice sticks or ribbon noodles depending on whether they are round or flat. Cook them in boiling water for 3–4 minutes until tender and once they are ready, drain in a colander under running cold water and rub them gently between your fingers so they do not stick together.

⌘ INGREDIENTS ⌘

- 2 tbsp peanut oil
- 8 oz pork steaks, cut into thin strips
- 1 green bell pepper, deseeded and sliced
- 1 Japone chili, deseeded and chopped
- 2 shallots, peeled and sliced
- 6 oz bean sprouts
- 6 oz shiitake mushrooms, quartered or sliced
- 8 oz raw tiger shrimp, peeled and deveined
- 11 oz flat rice noodles, cooked
- 4 finely sliced or shredded scallions, to garnish

1. Heat the oil in a wok, add the pork strips, and stir-fry over brisk heat for 4–5 minutes. Remove from the pan and set aside.

2. Add the bell pepper, shallots, and bean sprouts and stir-fry for 3 minutes. Add the mushrooms and shrimp and stir-fry for a further 2 minutes until the vegetables are starting to soften and the shrimp turn pink.

3. Return the pork to the pan, add the noodles, and pour on the sauce. Toss together over the heat until everything is well combined and piping hot. Sprinkle with the scallions and serve at once.

SERVES 4

CHICKEN WITH PINEAPPLE & THREE-FLAVOR SAUCE

This dish is known in Thailand as *Gai Tod Saporot*. It features a sauce that crops up in dishes all over the country, offering a balance of sour, sweet, and salty flavors. Add extra fire by adding chili sauce as a condiment.

⚜ INGREDIENTS ⚜

- 6 boneless chicken thighs, skinned and cut into pieces
- 4 scallions, trimmed and sliced
- 1 slice pineapple, cut into pieces
- 5 fl. oz chicken broth
- 4 kaffir lime leaves, sliced
- 2 tbsp peanut oil
- 2 cloves garlic, peeled and minced
- 1 tsp fresh ginger purée
- 1 medium cayenne chili, deseeded and chopped
- 2 shallots, peeled and finely chopped
- 2 tbsp soft brown sugar
- 1 tsp tamarind paste
- 1 tbsp fish sauce
- juice of 3 limes
- 4 tbsp peanut oil

1. To make the sauce, heat 2 tablespoons oil in a wok and fry the garlic, ginger purée, chili, and shallots over a low heat for 3 minutes. Add the sugar and cook until it caramelizes. Add the tamarind paste, fish sauce, and lime juice and remove from the heat.

2. Heat the remaining oil in a skillet and stir-fry the chicken in two batches for 1–2 minutes over a brisk heat. Remove and set aside.

3. Add the scallions and pineapple to the skillet and stir-fry for 1 minute. Transfer the scallions and pineapple to the three-flavor sauce in the wok, stir in the stock, and bring to a simmer. Lower the heat, add the chicken and lime leaves, and cook gently for 10 minutes. Serve on a bed of rice noodles.

SERVES 4

EGG NOODLES
WITH BEEF & VEGETABLES

VERY HOT

Thai egg noodles are the basis of this dish. They have a distinctive yellow color in contrast to the more commonly used white rice noodles. The shrimp paste used in this recipe is highly pungent, but do not let the odor put you off. Wise Thai cooks make sure their kitchen is well ventilated while they are cooking.

INGREDIENTS

- 10 oz dried, medium egg noodles
- 3 tbsp vegetable oil
- 2–3 small dried pasilla chilies, soaked in hot water, then ground
- 2 cloves garlic, finely chopped
- 1 tsp dried shrimp paste (optional)
- 10 oz round steak, thinly sliced
- 1 medium onion, thinly sliced
- 2 bird's eye chilies, chopped
- 7 oz bean sprouts
- 1 carrot, chopped
- 4 oz fresh spinach
- salt and freshly ground pepper
- 3 tbsp dark soy sauce and light soy sauce

1. In a large pan, bring a quantity of water to a boil, add the egg noodles, and cook for 4 minutes. Rinse under cold water and drain.

2. Heat the oil in a wok or skillet, and stir-fry the red chilies, garlic, and shrimp paste, if using. Add the beef and fry for 2–3 minutes or until cooked.

3. Add the onion, green chilies, bean sprouts, carrots, and spinach, stirring in the ingredients one by one. Season to taste with the salt and pepper.

4. Add the noodles, sprinkle over both soy sauces, and mix well. Divide the noodles among four plates and garnish with cilantro leaves and lime wedges. Serve immediately.

SERVES 4

DRINKS & SWEETS

MANDARIN, LEMONGRASS, CHILI & MINT JUICE

MILD SPICE

Adding chili to fruit juice might sound bizarre, but in small quantities it provides a flavor hit without excessive heat.

INGREDIENTS

- 4 mandarin oranges, peeled
- 1 lemongrass stalk, trimmed
- ½ a long, red chili, such as poblano or jalapeño, deseeded
- 5 fresh mint leaves

1. Put all the ingredients through a juice extractor. Pour into a glass and serve immediately.

SERVES 2

MEDIUM
SPICE

BANGKOK BLOODY MARY

The Bloody Mary hangover cure was created in 1921 in Paris, inspired by America's sweetheart, Mary Pickford. She had previously drunk a similar cocktail, so the new drink was named after her—"blood" depicting the tomato juice rather than any reflection on the lady herself!

⌁INGREDIENTS⌁

- 4 fl. oz tomato juice
- 2 fl. oz lemongrass-infused vodka
- 1 tsp sugar syrup
- ½ tsp hot chili sauce
- dash of Thai fish sauce
- ice cubes
- lemon or lime zest

1. Put the tomato juice, vodka, sugar syrup, hot chili sauce, and fish sauce in a tall glass over ice. Stir until all the ingredients are combined. Or, shake together in a cocktail shaker, and then pour into the glass over the ice. Garnish with a thin twist of lemon or lime zest.

SERVES 2

CHILI, AVOCADO & LEMON MUFFINS

Avocados contain a host of essential oils, vitamins, and minerals—all beneficial for the body's nervous system. A dash of chili adds a kick to really get you going!

INGREDIENTS

- 2 medium avocados, peeled and roughly chopped
- 1 tsp lemon juice
- 8 oz all-purpose flour
- pinch of salt
- 1 tbsp baking powder
- 1 tbsp Anaheim chili, deseeded and finely chopped
- 2 lightly beaten eggs
- 1 cup milk
- 4 tbsp extra virgin olive oil
- 4 tbsp sweet butter, melted
- 1½ tbsp grated lemon zest
- 1 tsp freshly ground pepper

1. Preheat the oven to 400°F (200°C). Grease a 12-cup muffin pan.

2. Place the avocado in a bowl with the lemon juice. Crush lightly with a fork. In a medium bowl, mix the flour, salt, baking powder, and chili. Beat the remaining ingredients together in a third large bowl. Add the flour mixture, stirring until nearly combined. Fold in the avocado. Do not overmix.

3. Spoon the mixture into the prepared pan. Bake for 20 minutes. Remove pan from the oven and cool for 5 minutes. Then remove the muffins and cool on a rack.

4. Store in an airtight container for up to 2 days or freeze for up to 3 months.

MAKES 1 DOZEN

MILD SPICE

CHOCOLATE & CHILI CUPCAKES

The Spanish *conquistadors* brought chocolate back from Mexico—inspiring this delicious combination of bittersweet chocolate and tingling chili.

ᴥ INGREDIENTS ᴥ

- 8 oz unsalted butter, softened
- 7 oz superfine sugar
- 6 oz self-rising flour
- 4 tbsp Dutch-process cocoa powder
- 1 tsp baking powder
- 4 eggs
- 2 tsp chipotle chili powder
- 3 ½ oz semisweet chocolate chips
- 3 oz unsweetened chocolate, melted
- 3 tbsp butter, melted
- 24 oz confectioners' sugar
- 1 tsp vanilla extract
- 4 tbsp milk

1. Preheat the oven to 350°F (175°C). Place 18 paper baking cups in muffin pans. Combine all the cupcake ingredients, except the chocolate chips, in a large bowl and beat with an electric mixer until smooth, about 2–3 minutes. Stir in the chocolate chips.

2. Spoon the batter into the cups. Bake for 20 minutes. Remove pans from the oven and cool for 5 minutes. Then remove the cupcakes and cool on a rack.

3. To make the frosting, blend the final 5 ingredients together in a food processor. Spread the frosting on the cooled cupcakes. Store unfrosted in an airtight container for up to 2 days.

MAKES 18

MEDIUM SPICE

VODKA, CHILI & CHOCOLATE CHIP CUPCAKES

Try using dark rum in this recipe to give these cupcakes a warm Caribbean feel.

⌐ INGREDIENTS ⌐

- 1 tbsp deseeded and finely chopped Anaheim chilies
- 3½ oz semisweet chocolate chips
- 3 tbsp vodka
- 8 oz sweet butter, softened
- 7 oz superfine sugar
- 8 oz self-rising flour
- 1 tsp baking powder
- 4 eggs
- 5 tbsp dark rum
- 2 tbsp light brown sugar

Makes 18

1. Soak the chilies and the chocolate chips in the vodka for 2 to 3 hours or overnight to soften them. Drain. Preheat the oven to 350°F (175°C). Place 18 paper baking cups in muffin pans. Combine all the remaining cupcake ingredients, except the rum and brown sugar, in a large bowl and beat with an electric mixer until smooth and pale, about 2 to 3 minutes. Stir in the chilies and chocolate chips. Spoon the batter into the cups. Bake for 20 minutes.

2. Dissolve the sugar in the rum over low heat. Simmer for 5 minutes. Remove pans from the oven. With a toothpick, prick 5 holes in each cupcake and pour the warm syrup over them. Then remove the cupcakes and cool on a rack.

3. Store in an airtight container for up to 3 days, or freeze for up to 3 months.

184 Sweet and spicy poached pears

MEDIUM SPICE

SWEET AND SPICY POACHED PEARS

Poached pears are given an Asian-style twist with this delicious recipe.

INGREDIENTS

- 2 cups white wine
- 4 cups water
- 1 vanilla bean, split lengthwise
- 1 bird's eye chili, bruised but not split
- 1 tbsp lemon juice
- 4 Bosc, Bartlett, or Conference pears, peeled and cored
- 1¼ cups sugar
- vanilla ice cream or goat cheese, to serve

1. In a saucepan, combine wine, water, vanilla bean, chili, and lemon juice. Simmer for 5 minutes.

2. Add pears to poaching liquid and poach for 8 minutes. Remove from liquid.

3. Continue to simmer syrup to reduce by one-half. Strain though a fine seive.

4. Serve the pears and syrup with a good-quality vanilla ice cream or, for a slightly more unusual twist, try serving with a slice of pungent goat cheese.

SERVES 2

MILD
SPICE

SPICY PAPAYA AND CHILI SMOOTHIE

Papaya is often paired with chili in Thai-style salads or relishes. This smoothie combines them both for a drink that is not too sweet, and packs a real punch!

INGREDIENTS

- 1 large papaya, chopped, peeled, and deseeded
- 8 fl. oz pineapple juice
- 4 fl. oz skim milk
- 4 oz sliced banana
- 4 ice cubes
- 1 red poblano chili, finely chopped and deseeded
- 1 tbsp honey
- juice of 1 fresh lime
- wedge of fresh lime, to serve
- mint leaves, to decorate

1. Combine all ingredients in blender. Purée until smooth and pour into 2 tall glasses. Decorate with mint leaves, and serve with a wedge of fresh lime.

SERVES 2

188 Mayan hot chocolate

MAYAN HOT CHOCOLATE

MEDIUM SPICE

Play Juliette Binoche in *Chocolat* and serve this to all your friends and family. But be warned—this is highly addictive!

INGREDIENTS

- 1⅔ cups milk
- 1 vanilla bean, split lengthwise
- 1 jalapeño chili, split with seeds removed
- 1 cinnamon stick
- 1 ½ oz bittersweet chocolate, grated

1. Simmer milk in a saucepan with the vanilla bean, cinnamon, and chili. Heat through for about 1 minute.

2. Whisk in grated chocolate, and continue to simmer until melted.

3. Remove from heat and let "steep" for another 10 minutes. Strain out the spices and serve.

SERVES 2

INDEX

190

PICTURE CREDITS

Alamy 25 blickwinkel/Alamy; 148 Bon Appetit/Alamy. **Getty Images** 6 B-L The Bridgeman Art Library/Getty Images. **iStock** 17; 21; 24; 32; 66; 69; 84; 93; 114; 121; 130; 147; 155; 162; 171. **Shutterstock** 7; 8; 9; 11; 12; 13; 14; 15; 16; 18; 19; 20; 22; 23; 27; 39; 43; 58; 60; 63; 64; 76; 89; 101; 109; 110; 135; 140; 144; 151; 163; 166; 184; 187. **Stockfood** 37 Baranowski, Andre/Stockfood America 40 Teubner Foodfoto/Stockfood America; 44 Borrelli, Joe/Stockfood America; 57 Plewinski, Antje/Stockfood America; 70 Plewinski, Antje/Stockfood America; 72 Brauner, M./Stockfood America; 83 Foodcollection/Stockfood America; 86 Garlick, Ian/Stockfood America; 98 Foodcollection/Stockfood America; 107 Nilsson, P./Stockfood America; 113 Morgenthaler, Walter/Stockfood America; 122 Nilsson, P./Stockfood America; 125 Wyatt, Rawdon/Stockfood America; 143 Rynio, J./Stockfood America; 152 Cazals, Jean/Stockfood America; 159 Kirchherr, Jo/Stockfood America; 160 FoodPhotogr. Eising/Stockfood America; 183 Fritz, Albert/Stockfood America; 188 Schardt, Wolfgang/Stockfood America.